# YOUR KNOWLEDGE HAS VALUE

- We will publish your bachelor's and master's thesis, essays and papers

- Your own eBook and book - sold worldwide in all relevant shops

- Earn money with each sale

## Upload your text at www.GRIN.com and publish for free

**Bibliographic information published by the German National Library:**

The German National Library lists this publication in the National Bibliography; detailed bibliographic data are available on the Internet at http://dnb.dnb.de .

**Imprint:**

Copyright © 2015 GRIN Verlag, Open Publishing GmbH
Print and binding: Books on Demand GmbH, Norderstedt Germany
ISBN: 978-3-668-06613-7

**This book at GRIN:**

http://www.grin.com/en/e-book/308134/process-mining-and-network-protocols

Matthias Leeb

# Process Mining and Network Protocols

**Probing the application of process mining techniques and algorithms to network protocols**

GRIN Publishing

**GRIN - Your knowledge has value**

Since its foundation in 1998, GRIN has specialized in publishing academic texts by students, college teachers and other academics as e-book and printed book. The website www.grin.com is an ideal platform for presenting term papers, final papers, scientific essays, dissertations and specialist books.

**Visit us on the internet:**

http://www.grin.com/

http://www.facebook.com/grincom

http://www.twitter.com/grin_com

# Process Mining And Network Protocols

## Probing the application of process mining techniques and algorithms to network protocols

### Diplomarbeit

zur Erlangung des akademischen Grades

### Diplom-Ingenieur/in

eingereicht von

### Matthias Leeb

im Rahmen des

Studienganges Information Security an der Fachhochschule St. Pölten

# Abstract

Process mining is the binding link between computational intelligence, data mining, process modeling and analysis. The thesis shows how this research discipline can be applied to network protocols and what the awards will be. Process mining is based on event data, logged by almost every information system. This event data is extracted, transformed and loaded into the process mining tool to discover, check conformance or enhance the underlying process based on observed behavior. Determining the significance of process mining in the field of network protocols and their control flow, finding the best possible algorithms and notation systems, clarifying the prerequisites and providing a proof of concept are the main achievements. Additionally other reasonable and beneficial applications, like mining an alternative protocol, dealing with a large amount of event data and estimations due to size of necessary event data, are investigated.

Matthias Leeb

# Contents

Matthias Leeb

# 1. Introduction

Process enhancement and conformance checking are often debated issues in many organizations and are in demand in a variety of application domains. Nowadays most processes are backed by or based on information systems. Solutions for Business Process Management (BPM) and Business Intelligence (BI) provide detailed information about the processes of an organization, mostly being limited to the "to-be" view, without the possibility to monitor or diagnose process execution or real behavior. On the other hand, data-mining techniques are too data-oriented to provide insights to the underlying end-to-end processes.

Every information system produces event logs, whether it is a webserver logging every request and the according answer or an Enterprise Resource Planning (ERP) software that dumps every transaction into continuously growing log files. In most cases these event logs are, if at all, used passively. They are only paid attention to, when there is an incident that has to be investigated or the auditor is asking for them. From the process miner's point of view this is a waste as event data can be used to discover the "as-is" process automatically and even compare it to the "to-be" process. This is where process mining jumps in, trying to unveil fact-based insight into processes by examining on real-life behavior.

## 1.1. Process Mining

Van der Aalst et al. define process mining in their manifest as follows:
"Process mining is a relatively young research discipline that sits between computational intelligence and data mining on the one hand, and process modeling and analysis on the other hand. The idea of process mining is to discover, monitor and improve real processes (i.e., not assumed processes) by extracting knowledge from event logs readily available in today's (information) systems."[79, p. 1]

Whether there already is a BPM or not, process mining is the technology to discover or enhance the processes or check them due to conformity based on event data. There are several tools and algorithms that support extracting and visualizing processes from event logs. Process Mining can be used in a large variety of application domains. The techniques are based on event data written by information systems.

The models describing processes can be discovered by extracting the audit trails of a WorkFlow Management (WFM) system or even the transaction logs of an ERP system. In addition to organizational relations and the manufacture of a product to its final disposal, processes mining can be used for monitoring the process and highlighting deviations to a predefined model or business rules, specified in the Sarbanes-Oxley Act (SOX).[24]

## 1.2. Business processes and network protocols

In order to understand (business) processes and network protocols, one needs to think about how they are defined and what characteristics both have. There are several definitions for *processes* and *business processes*. Hank Johansson defines a process as "a set of linked activities that take an input and transform it to create an output. Ideally, the transformation that occurs in the process should add value to the input and create an output that is more useful and effective to the recipient either upstream or downstream."[49].

Davenport defines a business process as a procedure to serve a customer or a market with a specified output. To reach this goal, a set of activities is structured and measured. The focus is on what is the input, how work is done and what output has to be produced, giving the process the structure.[10, p. 5] In conclusion, a process produces a defined set of result by following a series of logically related activities or tasks.[46]

**Protocols** can be seen as formal rules of behavior. It is unimportant if the object under observation is an international diplomatic meeting or a network communication. Protocols consist of sets of rules that minimize misunderstandings and tell everyone involved how to act or react in a certain situation.[43] As the above definitions show, there are similarities between business processes and network protocols. So why not try applying the process mining concepts to network protocols?

## 1.3. Vision

Discovering rarely used protocols, checking well known and defined protocols for conformance or providing different perspectives on protocols, e.g. on control flow, organization or time, for the purpose of enhancement seem to be viable and valuable accomplishments. Achieving these goals by observing network traffic would open the gates to monitoring and auditing at neuralgic points in networks, without the need for agents or additional modules in information systems to be supervised. The reverse engineering or conformance checking of protocols - either in a forensic approach or "live" - would lead to new opportunities for vendors of network security devices and services just as for auditors or consultants.

## 1.4. Idea, leading questions and strategy

The idea behind this thesis is to investigate which process mining concepts, types and perspectives are applicable to network protocols. As tools for process mining, the open-source software *ProM*[78, pp.265-269] and the commercial tool *Disco*[50] are two exemplary representatives. Prom is also available as an extension for the data mining tool *Rapidminer*[45] named *RapidProM*[40]. These tools make it possible to elaborate on and explore event logs and processes in many ways and from different points of view.

Process mining has already arrived in big institutions from several domains, both private and public sector. Over the past years the list of talks at the *Process Mining Camp*[51][52][53][54] shows, that banks, financial auditors, business analysts, statistical researchers and advisors already put process mining into practice for many different purposes. The benefit for information security and management may include

- reverse engineering or reengineering network protocols,

- checking conformance of communication or

- enhancing the performance or compliance of communication

to name but a few. To accomplish these goals, the information has to be extracted from plain network communication and prepared for the mining process. Additionally the visualization is an issue to elaborate on.

Concerning to focus on control flow of protocols this leads to the following set of questions:

1. Which perspectives and types of process mining are significant to network protocols? - This questions will be answered via literature research and investigating information security topics and questions.

2. Which process mining algorithms and notation systems are viable? - This question will be answered through literature research. Finding "the weapons of choice" for process mining network protocols is the main intention here.

3. What are the requirements and prerequisites to process captured network traffic with process mining tools? - This question will be tackled by a systematic literature research followed by a empirical proof of concept. Finding a procedure to bring the captured or live network traffic to a form, that can be processed by process mining tools like *ProM*(see [25]) is the goal to accomplish.

4. What are reasonable applications of process mining in the field of network protocols? - In this section the methods discussed earlier in this thesis will be applied to concrete protocols.

## 1.5. Outcome

The findings in this thesis show, that many questions around network protocols and their discovery or conformance can be answered. The combinations of perspectives - control flow, organization, cases and timing or frequencies - and types - play-in, play-out and replay - deliver a wide variety of applications. The properties and qualities of logs, the mining algorithm, the model and notation systems are crucial as they, each on its own, can avoid reaching a satisfactory outcome of the mining procedure. The freedom of choice is additionally narrowed by the few algorithms implemented in process mining tools. For control-flow mining the Fuzzy miner seems to be a good formula, while choosing the mining tool is a matter of one's goals and technical skills. Disco is the tool of choice, if usability, speed and beautiful visualization are expected. ProM is the more "scientific and technical" tool, offering flexibility and export options for further processing.

Both tools expect eXtensible Event Stream (XES) as input format and the quality of logs is influenced primarily by noise and incompleteness.

The Extract, Transform, Load (ETL) procedure has two major hurdles to overcome:

- Bridging the operational, syntactic and semantic gap between the data source - in this case network captures - and the process mining tools.

- Addressing the above mentioned quality criteria for logs.

Developing an ETL procedure is a complex process and time-consuming. For bridging the above mentioned gap, deep understanding of both the network and the process mining domain is necessary. For a proof of concept the ETL procedure was automated for control-flow mining of Transmission Control Protocol (TCP) by scripts.

For mining the Hypertext Transfer Protocol (HTTP) and dealing with big network captures, the ETL scripts got adapted and enhanced.

To predict the minimum size of a training set or estimating when enough logs are gathered to mine a proper process model, a metric, based on the average information gain over a growing number of cases, is introduced and statistical analysis are carried out.

## 1.6. Structure of thesis

The structure of this theses reflects the leading questions listed in section 1.4. Following this introduction, chapter 2 gives an overview of process mining and its related topics to find out, how the techniques, perspectives and methods of process mining work out and if they can be applied and lead to benefits in the domain of network protocols and specific questions can be answered.

Chapter 3 is dedicated to the properties and quality of event data, algorithms, the process model and the corresponding notation systems. By literature research the answer to the question of the best combination of the above mentioned dimensions is elaborated.

The prerequisites and the necessary preprocessing to start process mining network protocols are covered in chapter 4. The operational, syntactic and semantic gap between the two domains is bridged by the ETL procedure and automated with a script.

Chapter 5 shows the so far derived expertise and experiences in action. The proof of concept shows the application of process mining to elaborate on the control flow of the TCP.

Chapter 6 highlights more interesting possibilities of application. The ETL process is adapted to the HTTP. To be able to deal with bigger amounts of event data the ETL process for TCP is enhanced. As a culmination of this thesis the problem of finding the adequate amount of event data is addressed.

Final conclusions and an outlook on future work are the subjects of the last two chapters.

# 2. Process Mining and related topics

This chapter provides all basic information and an explanation of the technical environment to address the connections between network traffic and its protocols on the one hand, and the tools and algorithms of process mining on the other.

The first gap to close is the one between the network traffic and the tool that is used for process mining.

## 2.1. The BPM life-cycle

To understand process mining we need a basic understanding of the BPM life-cycle shown in figure 2.1.

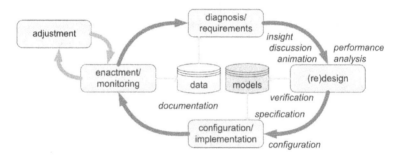

Figure 2.1.: BPM life-cycle [78, p. 8]

The different phases of managing a business process describe a circle. The phases are:

- Design / Redesign: Here the process is designed as a model.

- Configuration / Implementation: Depending on the existence and maturity level of the WFM or BPM system the model is transformed into a running system.

- Enactment / Monitoring: In this phase the process can be fired at any time and is monitored by the management. The gathered data is the foundation for future enhancements and adaptions.

- Adjustment: Minor changes can be made in the adjustment phase. A redesign of the process is not possible here.

- Requirements / Diagnosis: The process is evaluated here and requirements for a redesign are derived from the monitoring data or external motivations like change of policies or new laws.

While the enactment/monitoring and the diagnosis/requirements phase are more data centric, the primary focus during the (re-) design and configuration/implementation phase is on the process models. However the diagnosis/requirements phase is mostly not supported in a managed way so the life-cycle is only started again, when there are severe problems or external changes take place.

BPM tools have limitations when it comes to supporting the the diagnosis and (re)design phase. The root cause is the missing connection between design and reality and the resulting inability to compare them automatically (see conclusions in [2]). Process mining offers a way to discover, monitor and improve real processes by analyzing the data recorded by information systems. These more factual information derived from event logs can also trigger the BPM life-cycle.[78, pp. 7-8]

## 2.2. Process modeling notations

Process modeling deals with the activity of representing processes. The visualization can take place in different notations. Each of the notations has its strengths and weaknesses, most of the time resulting from a trade-off between the ease of use,the universal usability and the field of application.

As BPM and Process-Aware Information System (PAIS) (see [17, pp. 5-8] for definition) are depending on process models, the modeling of business and other processes is mission critical. The processes are described in terms of activities, that have to be ordered logically and chronologically correctly. The notations have to provide the opportunity to accomplish this requirement. A more detailed view of the notations and their properties and usability is given in section 3.2.

## 2.3. Positioning process mining

Process mining creates the links between the processes and their data and the process model. Figure 2.2 shows these links.

Information systems produce a vast amount of event data that is written - most often unstructured - into one or more tables or plain text files. To do proper process mining the extraction and aggregation of the event data is mission critical. Each event logged should consist of the following information:

- Index/Timestamp: Sequential order of events is unambiguous.

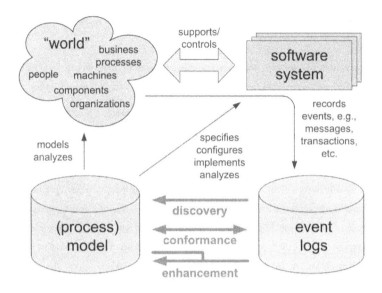

Figure 2.2.: Positioning of the three main types of process mining [78, p. 9]

- Activity: A well defined step in the process.

- Case: A process id that helps to distinguish the process instances from each other.

With these pieces of information the control flow of a process can be extracted from the event log. Depending on the purpose of the process mining, additional information can be stored for other or more comprehensive analysis.[78, pp. 8-9]

## 2.4. Process models, analysis and limitations

Process models allow many approaches[78, p. 6] to look at processes:
For better *insight* the modeler is triggered to view the process from various angles. A model also forms a basis for a proper *discussion* with stakeholders, while *documenting* a process makes it possible to train other people to a certain procedure or policy, or to achieve a certification. The process model can be used as a baseline for *analyzing systems* or procedures due to *failures or unconformities*. Techniques like simulation can be used to examine the *performance* of a process. Also animation, specification and configuration can be done by using process models.

### 2.4.1. Model-based process analysis

As mentioned in section 2.4, verification and performance analysis are two main issues in process analysis. As the focus of this thesis is on control flow, verification is more important as it is concerned with the correctness of a process[78, pp. 52].

**Verification**  Two possible tasks for verification are

- checking the soundness of a process and

- the comparison of two models.

"Soundness" means in effect, that from each and every state of a process the end state must be reachable. Anomalies just like deadlocks[1] and livelocks[2] have to be eliminated as they prevent reaching the end state.

Exemplary tools for verification are Woflan[1] and the workflow system Yet Another Workflow Language (YAWL)[31].

**Example**  For better legibility a example, with a given *Petri net* (see appendix A.1 for details) in form of a *Petri Net Markup Language (PNML)* file and the tool *Workflow Petri Net Designer (WoPeD)* (see appendix B.11), will explain how soundness can be tested automatically. Figure 2.3 describes the Petri net under examination. The process shows the handling of requests for compensation and is mined from cases 1 and 4 from event data in [78, p. 13] leading to the model in [78, p. 15].

WoPeD is able to do a semantical analysis (found in tab *Analyze → Semantical analysis*) on a given Petri net.

**Result**  The result of this analysis is shown in figure 2.4. Some statistics about places, transitions and arcs are listed in the bottom half. More important here is the analysis of *soundness* (explained in section 2.4.1). WoPeD confirms the soundness of the Petri net, illustrated by the green checkmark.

### 2.4.2. Limitations

The verification analysis only makes sense, if it is based on proper process models. There are several problems based on "a lack of alignment between hand-made models and reality"[78, p. 57]. The model is useless if it is based on wrong conclusions or represents a *too idealized* version of the reality. What

---

[1]A situation in which two or more competing actions are each waiting for the other to finish, and thus neither ever does.

[2]Similar to a deadlock, except that the states of the processes involved in the livelock constantly change with regard to one another, none progressing.

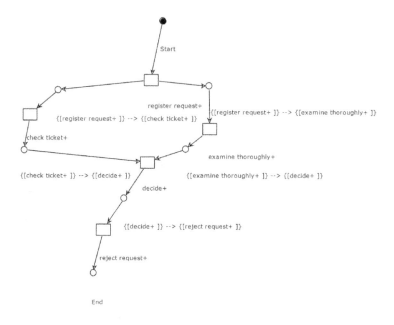

Figure 2.3.: Exemplary Petri net

Figure 2.4.: Semantic analysis results

quality criteria models have to fulfill and how they are measured and quantified is described in section 3.4. According to [78, p. 57] "Process mining aims to address these problems by establishing a direct connection between the models and actual low-level event data about the process."[78, p. 57]

## 2.5. Perspectives of process mining

When talking about processes and their variations of execution, the *control-flow perspective* is taken up and the ordering and logical sequence of activities and the possible or intended variants of execution come to the fore. A comprehensive example for this perspective is given in section 2.6.

Additionally there is a non-exhaustive number of other perspectives[78, p. 11] that have to be considered.

**Organization** The focus is on the resources in a process and how they interact. Actors shall be structured in terms of roles or organizational matters. As activities are put into relation to resources, interesting fields like work distribution, work patterns or roles can be investigated.[78, pp. 221-230]

Let us assume, a company policy saying, that for each and every activity in the business processes there have to be at least two persons who are able to successfully do the activity. The organizational mining perspective could answer this question and show every activity that has been performed by only one person and highlight the need for action.

**Cases** The focus is on the characterization of process executions based on certain values of properties. This perspective is all about the mining of decision trees.[78, pp. 234-237]

Assuming to have a process with a XOR-split, this perspective tries to tell why a certain path in the process execution happens. For this reason the event log has to conclude the decisive factors as a property.

**Time** This perspective highlights all timing and frequency related topics of processes.[78, pp. 230-233]

This perspective can answer questions about service levels. An example could be the proof or ensurance that a certain response time or time to repair is provided to a company's customers.

Another purpose could be the detection of bottlenecks. With this perspective wait times before execution could put a highlight on congestions in processes.

## 2.6. Types of process mining

There are three types of process mining, namely

- *Discovery,*

- *Conformance* and

- *Enhancement.*

The types of process mining describe the relation between the process model and event data and how they can be translated into each other or checked for conformance. Event data has to contain certain properties to be able to do process mining. Event data will be discussed in section 3.1, however an exemplary event log could look like table 2.1, showing some remarkable characteristics. Each event is described by a case ID, an event ID and an activity. This is the minimal requirement to mine a process model. The case id is the identifier for an instance of the process. The event id has to be a unique identifier within an instance of a process. Either the events are consecutively numbered or the event ID is a timestamp. Both options help to avoid confusion due to the chronological order of events when two executions of the same process are overlapping. The activity represents a step during the execution of an instance.

| Case ID | Event ID | Activity |
|:---:|:---:|:---:|
| 1 | 101 | Register request |
| 1 | 103 | Examine thoroughly |
| 1 | 104 | Check ticket |
| 1 | 108 | Decide |
| 1 | 110 | Reject request |
| 2 | 102 | Register request |
| 2 | 105 | Check ticket |
| 2 | 106 | Examine casually |
| 2 | 107 | Decide |
| 2 | 109 | Pay compensation |
| ... | ... | ... |

Table 2.1.: Exemplary event log (extracted from [78, p. 13])

The following sections provide an overview of the methods and the types of process mining they are used for.

## 2.6.1. Play-in

When doing play-in the goal is to derive the process model from real behavior described by raw event data. As figure 2.5 describes, there is no need to do process modeling, because the model is inferred from the event data by a process mining algorithm. The features and properties of these process mining algorithms will be considered in section 3.3.

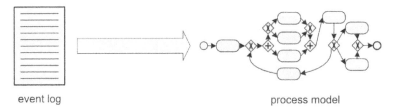

event log                                    process model

Figure 2.5.: Play-in [78, p. 19]

When doing play-in, the process model is inferred from behavior. The mission critical part in this procedure is finding a process model that represents - and represents only - the recorded traces in the event log. This type of process mining is used for discovery purposes.

**Inferring a process model**

Based on the event log in table 2.1 case 1 results in the process model shown in figure 2.6.

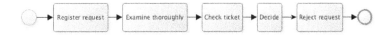

Figure 2.6.: Process model of Case 1

When investigating case 2, another variation of the process appears. Hence the *Examine* and the *Check ticket* activity change their order of occurrence. There, the order of execution is irrelevant and they can be parallelized. In addition, the activity *Examine casually* takes the place of the activity "Examine thoroughly" so these activities are executed either or. After the *Decision* the request is either rejected or compensation is payed. This leads to the process model in figure 2.7.

Assuming that there the event log contains more cases, the model may need to be extended again until all recorded cases are represented by the model.

Matthias Leeb                                                                                    13

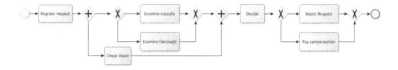

Figure 2.7.: Process model for case 1 and 2

## Discovery

The procedure described above is call *discovery* and can be performed without any a-priori information. Assuming that the event log contains sufficient and comprehensive example executions of the process to be discovered, this leads to a, for example, Petri net describing the process steps. Discovery is used, when there is no precedent information about processes.

## 2.6.2. Play-out

The basic idea with play-out is to derive behavior from an already existing model.

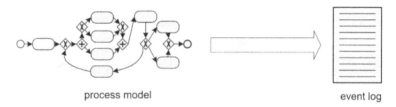

process model          event log

Figure 2.8.: Play-out [78, p. 19]

Executions of the modeled process are simulated. The goal is to *play-out* the complete process model and find every possible path of execution and scenario that is foreseen by the model. The range of possible scenarios ranges from 1 - when there are no optional paths - to infinite, when there is a loop within the process model.

## Simulation / Verification

When building an information system or simulating it based on process models, play-out is the thing to do. Verification, e.g. for the purposes of model checking, is also an application domain for this type of process mining.[78, pp. 18-19]

## 2.6.3. Replay

This type of process mining needs both, the event log and a process model. As figure 2.9 shows, the reality, represented by an event log, is *replayed* on top of the process model.

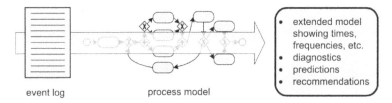

event log          process model

• extended model
  showing times,
  frequencies, etc.
• diagnostics
• predictions
• recommendations

Figure 2.9.: Replay [78, p. 19]

Replay can be used for the following purposes[78, pp. 19]:

• Conformance checking: Deviations of the log and the underlying process model can be detected and investigated by replaying the log and inspect the traces that show the deviation.

• Extending the model with frequencies and temporal information: To figure out which parts of the model are frequently used and tend to be bottlenecks one can consider the timestamps and the number of executions. As of the main focus of this thesis is the control flow, this will no be further examined.

• Constructing predictive models: In some cases the execution time , e.g. when service level agreements or guaranteed response times come into play, is relevant. Through replaying logs on the process model one can learn to predict completion time from any state of the process. Again this is not about the control flow an therefore not relevant in this thesis.

• Operational support: This can be accomplished by *live* replay during the execution. While executing the process on top of a model, deviations or other flaws can be detected and give the opportunity to influence the current execution. Focus of this technique can be, among others, the control flow.

### Conformance checking

To give a concrete example, the following assumption describes a situation, where the conformance check highlights a flaw.

| Case ID | Event ID | Activity |
|---------|----------|----------|
| ... | ... | ... |
| 3 | 110 | Register request |
| 3 | 111 | Examine casually |
| 3 | 112 | Check ticket |
| 3 | 113 | Decide |
| 3 | 114 | Reinitiate request |
| 3 | 115 | Examine thoroughly |
| 3 | 116 | Check ticket |
| 3 | 117 | Decide |
| 3 | 118 | Pay compensation |
| ... | ... | ... |

Table 2.2.: Additional event (extracted from [78, p. 13])

**Assumption**  In addition to the cases in table 2.1 there is another case shown in table 2.2. When replaying case 3 on top of the model in figure 2.7 one can see, that the event with the ID 114 is not possible with this model and therefore seen as a deviation and in case of a conformance check it is bound to fail. If the behavior represents a valid use case, the model is *incomplete*.

# 2.7. Discussion

The leading question of this discussion is the significance of the types of process mining. The following paragraphs will elaborate on ideas and specific applications of process mining methods and types on network protocols. Additionally, a preview of the estimated advantages and benefits is given.

### 2.7.1. Discovery

**Assumption 1**  A news company runs a webserver providing news of several domains, e.g. politics, sports, culture to name but a few. The marketing wants to know:

- How do visitors of the website navigate?

- Which domains are the most visited or visited first?

- How much time do visitors spend on the website?

All these questions can be answered through discovery techniques and mining of the control flow. The TCP and HTTP packet headers contain every bit of information, which is needed to answer the above questions. This can serve as a basis for further investigations or profiling visitors of the website.

**Assumption 2** A less widely used TCP-based network protocol should be investigated and reverse engineered. The packet headers contain the control characters and words.

The control flow of the protocol can be mined and visualized with process mining techniques. A potential attacker could gain deeper understanding of the protocol as a basis for attacks.

### 2.7.2. Conformance

**Assumption 1** When thinking of an Intrusion Prevention System (IPS), ensuring the correct control flow of the network protocol is a main task. Deviations from the standardized behavior could be a pointer towards a possible intruder break-in, trying to exploit a weakness of the protocol.

Replaying the observed behavior an top of a nominal model can highlight these deviations.

**Assumption 2** If certain activities in the expected control flow are missing or malformed, this could point to a weak or misinterpreted implementation of a network protocol.

Again replaying the observed behavior an top of a nominal model during a test can highlight these deviations.

### 2.7.3. Enhancement

The goal of enhancement is to extend or repair an existing process model based on observed real-life behavior. Enhancement comes into play, when the model does not cover every aspect of reality. As network protocols are well defined or even standardized, enhancement plays a minor role in this context. All behavior not agreeing with standards has to be classified as a deviation.

## 2.8. Findings

As described in section 2.7 there is a plethora of application opportunities for control-flow focused process mining due to network protocols promising better insight in this field. How logs need to be prepared is described in chapter 4 while chapter 5 shows a proof of concept and how ideas can effectively be put into practice.

Besides the control-flow perspective the other perspectives listed in 2.5 can also be taken in to account and combined arbitrarily with process mining types. This opens a wide variety opportunities to look at network protocols. Specific questions that require observing other characteristics of the behavior of a network protocol can be answered with these approaches.

The organizational perspective can provide a understanding which computer systems interact and reveal key players in a network. Taking the case perspective makes it possible to understand in which variations the protocol is commonly used and examine on them. Often protocols also contain restrictions due to timing and frequencies which can be elaborated by taking the time perspective into consideration.

# 3. Properties and quality

There are three key components in the field of process mining, namely the event data, the process model - pictured using a notation framework - and the mining algorithms. All these components have to have certain properties and fulfill certain minimum requirements regarding quality.

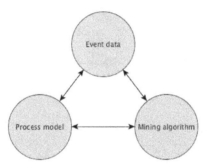

Figure 3.1.: Event, model and algorithm

Each component depends on the properties of the others as figure 3.1 shows. The following sections will explain the properties and quality criteria of the components and elaborate on the inter-dependencies. Another important thing to keep in mind is the representational bias. The notation system (e.g. workflow nets, petri nets et al.) of the process model has to be able to represent every aspect the mining algorithm is capable of discovering and vice versa. The following sections deal with this issue.

## 3.1. Event data

Event data is logged in many different forms and formats. Almost all information systems include a log mechanism but the implementations vary very widely. As most common forms plain text files, databases and datawarehouses should be mentioned. Figure 3.2 shows a generic structure most event logs of PAIS follow.

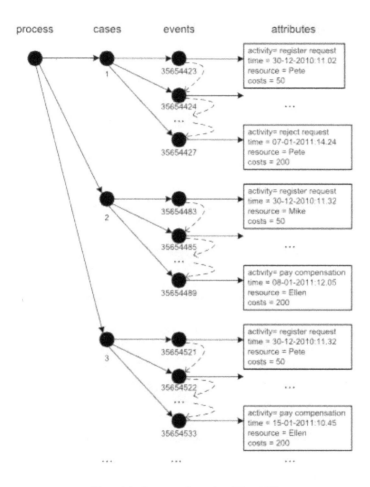

Figure 3.2.: Structure of event logs[78, p. 100]

The process is the hierarchically highest instance in this structure. Examples for a *process* could be a business sales process or a service provided by a server (e.g. a running Apache webserver[27]). *Cases* are instances of a process, identified by a primary designator (e.g. by a PID on a Linux server[5]). A case consists of one or more events, whereas the event consists of attributes that described what and when it happened.

This leads to the smallest set of information to do process mining assuming, that the event log consists of events of only one process:

A *case id* is necessary to distinguish several instances of a process. *Events* belong to a certain case. The *chronological order* of events is crucial to process mining. In most cases this is accomplished by a timestamp or a continuous counter.

As activities often last longer, they run through the so called *transitional life-cycle*. The stages of an activity are represented by an additional attribute that could take on values like *start, suspend, resume* or *complete*.[78, pp. 139-140]

### 3.1.1. Quality criteria and checks

The main quality criteria of event data are noise and incompleteness. the following subsections describe these criteria and point to possible checks to measure and quantify them.

#### Noise

If the event log contains rare and infrequent behavior not representative for the typical behavior of the process, this is called noise. Noise are exceptional events rather than incorrectly logged events. The discovery algorithm can not distinguish incorrect logging from exceptional events. It is therefore the responsibility of the human to judge and to do proper pre- and postprocessing of the extracted event log and avoid incorrect logging at an early stage.[78, p. 148]

#### Incompleteness

If the event log contains too few events to be able to discover some of the underlying control-flow structures, this is called incompleteness.[78, p. 149] For process mining a *big-enough* log is mission critical.

#### Checks

For quantifying how serious the above mentioned criteria have to be taken, the log can be inspected by cross-validation. When applying the *k-fold cross-validation* to a log, the data is split into e.g. 10 subsets and each is validated against the others as [78, pp. 85-88] and [78, pp. 149-150] describe.

### 3.1.2. Extensible event stream

Among the forms of event logs there is no generally acknowledged format. While its main focus is on process mining, XES tries to handle the above challenges and follows four guiding principles namely simplicity, flexibility, extensibility and expressivity. This implies, that only elements appearing in every event log are explicitly defined, while the others are optional attributes.[42, p. 1]

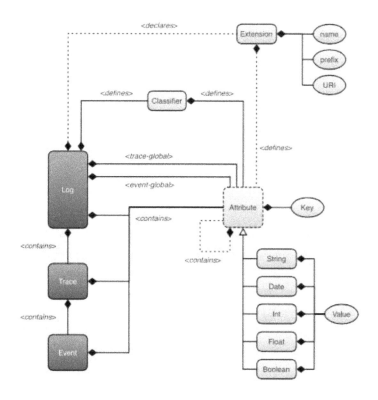

Figure 3.3.: Meta model of XES[78, p. 109]

Figure 3.3 shows the XES meta-model. This leads to a exemplary syntax as shown in listing 3.1.

```
<?xml version=" 0" encoding=" " ?>
```

```
<log xes.version="   " xes.features="             " xmlns="
                    ">
  <extension name="        " prefix="         " uri="
                    "/>
  <extension name="     " prefix="      " uri="
                    "/>
  <global scope="       ">
    <string key="            " value="  "/>
  </ global>
  <global scope="       ">
    <string key="            " value="  "/>
    <date key="            " value="
      >
    <string key="        " value="  "/>
  </ global>
  <classifier name="         " keys="            "/>
  <classifier name="        " keys="              "/>
  <float key="             " value="        "/>
  <trace>
  <string key="          " value="            "/>
    <event>
      <string key="          " value="             "/>
      <string key="        " value="       "/>
      <date key="            " value="
        "/>
      <int key="         " value="    ">
        <boolean key="          " value="      "/>
      </int>
    </event>
      <event>
        <string key="            " value="             "/>
        <string key="        " value="     "/>
        <date key="            " value="
```

```
+02:00"/>
      </event>
    </trace>
</log>
```

Listing 3.1: Exemplary XES file (from [42, p. 9])

The XES file starts with defining the eXtensible Markup Language (XML) version and the encoding. At the start of the actual log in the second line, the XES version and the used features and extensions are listed. The structure of each trace and event is defined and classifiers are named. Then the actual trace (containing two events) starts and is notated in the above defined way until the log is closed.

## 3.2. Notation frameworks

When doing process discovery and focusing on the control flow, the results of the mining algorithm need to be visualized in some way. This task should lead from the output of a mining algorithm to a process model that can be presented in several notations. According to [78, pp. 31] there are many process modeling notations, e.g. *transition systems, petri nets, workflow nets* and *YAWL*, just to name a few. Process Mining tools offer options to convert one into another as table 3.1 shows.

| Notation | → | Notation |
|---|---|---|
| Process Tree | → | Petri Net |
| Petri Net | → | Business Process Model and Notation (BPMN) |
| Heuristics Net | → | Petri Net |

Table 3.1.: Conversion of Process Modeling notations provided by RapidProM

A key factor is, that the notation system is able to represent concurrency and loops in a practical way. The transition system notation is not able to do this, which leads to the "state explosion"-problem as described in [78, p. 33] and is therefore unsuitable for mining non-linear processes and network protocols in particular. Other relevant challenges for both algorithms and notations are addressed in section 3.3.3.

## 3.3. Evaluation of algorithms

There are already several algorithms aiding the process of *Process Mining*. Algorithms like the $\alpha$-*Algorithm*[78, pp.129-139], the *ILP-Miner*[88], the *frequency abstraction miner*[18], the *fuzzy miner*[19] and others[20] can be used for control flow discovery.

Choosing a proper mining algorithm is a difficult task. The following sections explain the main obstacles that have to be overcome.

### 3.3.1. Problem statement

As mentioned in the abstracts of [69] and [70] the process mining algorithms are under constant and rapid development. On the other hand there is no "common means of assessing the quality of models discovered by these algorithms". This makes the decision towards a process mining algorithm non-trivial. The position paper [69] mentions the following obstacles, without any claim to comprehensiveness:

- Bridging the gap between different modeling languages.

- Defining good validation criteria for the process model.

- Defining good metrics for the quality of a process model.

**Discussion**   Several efforts and approaches towards these challenges ([81], [82] and [78, pp. 210-211]) have already been made. All these attempts require a reference model as a basis. Taking this as a fact, these approaches cannot be used in the context of this thesis, as there is no petri net or an in any other way notated reference model defined in neither the TCP standard[63] and nor in others.

### 3.3.2. What "Disco" does

In addition to the basic information about this commercial process mining tool in appendix B.1, information about the mode of operation is mentioned in [66]. Discos miner is based on the *Fuzzy miner*. The main features are the "seamless process simplification" realized via slide bars, that allow a granular setting for activities and paths. The activity slide bar allows the fading out of rarer activities and the paths slide bar does the same for less likely used execution paths of the process. This "map metaphor"-approach allows different levels of abstraction of the process map. The visualization options allow to focus on several metrics regarding frequency and performance.

### 3.3.3. Challenges for algorithms and notation systems

In the context of process mining there is no prior knowledge of the process and the underlying thoughts are unknown. There are certain situations where correct discovery and visualization is a real challenge and it is not obvious what is the valid representation has to look like.

Control-flow focused process mining algorithms[20] have to cope with challenges, e.g. concurrency[78, p. 15], short loops[78, pp.137], loops, frequencies[78, p. 20, pp.137], silent transitions[78, p. 139] and indirect dependencies[78, pp. 139], just to mention a few. The process mining algorithms are constantly evolving. As there are no common means of assessing the quality of the models discovered by the algorithms and the rapid development, choosing the right algorithm is an additional challenge.

**Concurrency, short loops and loops**   The term *concurrency* refers to activities, that happen in parallel. The log shows them in any possible order. *Loops* and *short loops* (length of one or two activities) describe a sequence of activities that is repeated non-predictably often. This implies that each sequence of activities - either concurrent or looped - leads to a separate path in the process model, if the algorithm cannot detect them and the notation system does not have the capability of AND and OR splits and joins(e.g. transition system). This is also known as the *state explosion* problem[78, p. 33].

### 3.3.4. Categorization of process mining algorithms

Although there is a wide variety of algorithms and derivatives, the underlying basic modes of operation allow sorting the process mining algorithms into four categories.

**Abstraction-based algorithms (class A)**   The abstraction-based algorithms[14, pp. 7-9], also known as $\alpha$-series algorithms, as most of them are derivatives of the $\alpha$ algorithm[78, pp. 129-138], mine in three phases. During the abstraction phase, pairs consisting of an activity and the succeeding activity are extracted from each trace of the event data. With this set of log-based ordering relations, the induction phase is entered to induce advanced ordering relations like splits and joins (both AND and XOR), invisible tasks and duplicate tasks, based on heuristic rules. In the final construction phase, the advanced ordering relations are put together assuming, that there is at least one relation between two activities to connect them via a transition arc.

As outlined in [14, p. 9] the heuristic rules are not effective enough and the special constructs (e.g. non-free-choices, duplicate tasks and invisible tasks) make it impossible to mine *sound* WorkFlow net

(WF-net) with abstraction-based algorithms.

**Heuristic-based algorithms (class H)**   The strength of heuristic-based algorithms[78, pp. 163-168][14, pp. 9-10] is based on the fact, that it takes the frequency of ordering relations into account to derive the advanced ordering relations. This results in the ability to deal with noise (see section 3.1.1). The thresholds, above which the frequency of the casual relations between two activities are considered in the process model, can be adjusted by the user. Despite *duplicate tasks* and some *non-free-choices* (also known as *indirect dependencies*) the heuristic-based mining algorithm can cope with all common constructs in process models.

**Search-based algorithms (class S)**   The search-based algorithms[78, pp. 169-172][14, pp. 10-11] extend the heuristic approach in a way, that they take the direct successors and predecessors and their successors and predecessors into account. The *fitness* of these sequences is compared to decide which sequence is represented in the resulting model. The four quality dimensions (explained in section 3.4) have to be balanced and can be influenced by the user.

**Region-based algorithms (class R)**   Process discovery with region-based algorithms is a two-step procedure. During the first step, a transition system has to be learned (see [78, pp. 174-177]). As transition systems tend to be unnecessarily complicated (*state explosion*, see 3.3.3), a Petri net is synthesized in a second step. A more compact Petri net has to be found, by detecting concurrency, based on the *theory of regions*[7][16], in the structures of the initial transition system. This task can be accomplished by using state-based ([78, pp. 177-180]) or language-based regions ([78, pp. 180-183]). Region-based algorithms have problems dealing with noise and incompleteness, due to their mode of operation.

**Findings**

The reflections above show, that each technique has its own weaknesses. As outlined in [78, pp. 186-187], only few discovery algorithms are useful for practical applications, namely fuzzy mining (discussed in detail in section 3.3.6), heuristic mining and genetic mining.

### 3.3.5. Algorithms and plug-ins for control-flow discovery

There are several plug-ins that assist control-flow discovery as shown at [20]. Table 3.2 shows this list and the process mining tools having these plug-ins implemented.

| Algorithm | Disco | ProM | RapidProM | Class | Model type |
|---|:---:|:---:|:---:|:---:|---|
| α[78] | - | ✓ | ✓ | A | Petri net |
| α++[86] | - | - | - | A | Petri net |
| Parikh Language-based Region miner[16] | - | - | - | R | Petri net |
| Region miner[16] | - | - | - | R | Petri net |
| Tsinghua-alpha algorithm plugin[85] | - | - | - | A | Petri net |
| Petrify mining[80] | - | ✓ | ✓ | - | Petri net |
| Duplicate Tasks GA plugin[59] | - | - | - | S | Heuristic net |
| Genetic algorithm plugin[59][58] | - | - | ✓ | S | Heuristic net |
| Heuristics miner[83][84] | - | ✓ | ✓ | H | Heuristic net |
| Frequency abstraction miner[18] | - | - | - | - | Fuzzy model |
| Fuzzy Miner[19] | ✓ | ✓ | ✓ | - | Fuzzy model |
| Finite State Machine (FSM) miner | - | - | - | - | Transition system |
| k-RI Miner | - | - | - | - | Transition system |
| Multi-phase Macro Plugin[15] | - | - | - | - | Event-driven Process Chain |
| DWS mining plug-in[39] | - | - | - | - | Other |
| Workflow patterns miner[38] | - | - | - | - | Other |

Table 3.2.: Table of control-flow plugins(from [20]) in process mining tools

## Discussion

To find out the plug-ins that assist the goal of this thesis - discovering the control flow of a network protocol - the findings in [14, pp. 6]) and the availability of the corresponding plug-in are taken into account. The α-algorithm has unacceptable limitations when it comes to loops, non-free-choices invisible tasks and duplicate tasks and is therefore not suitable for mining network protocols (see [57, pp. 394] for further details). Also the other α-based algorithms only show insufficient improvements here(see e.g. [6, pp. 27-28]). The mining algorithms based on the "theory of regions" (*Region miners*, see [16]), also have shortcomings at invisible and duplicate tasks. The *Petrify mining* plug-in can convert a transition system into a petri net[80]. ProM and RapidProM both are able to convert other initial notations into petri nets. As this is not the focus of this thesis, the plug-in is kept aside. While the *Genetic Algorithm* is not able to cope with duplicate tasks, the *Duplicate Tasks Genetic Algorithm* does not show this or other weaknesses mentioned above, but there is no plug-in available. The *Heuristics miner* is not able to mine duplicate tasks correctly and struggles with non-free-choices. A plug-in for ProM and Rapid-ProM exists. "The Frequency Abstraction Miner is a plug-in for ProM which enables to mine processes in a successive and user-definable fashion, zooming to the desired level of precision and detail. The importance of events and transition is evaluated by frequency, i.e. more frequently observed artifacts are considered more important."[18] When mining the control flow of a network protocol, one has to gain a complete picture of the behavior. Abstraction does not assist this intention. The *FSM* miner is neither available as a plug-in nor ready to mine AND and OR splits and joins. The *k-RI* miner produces a transition system as output model type. The *transition system notation* has the same shortcomings, leading to the problems described in section 3.2. The *Multi-phase Macro*(see [15]) plug-in is no more available in ProM and is therefore not taken into account. The *Disjunctive Workflow Schema (DWS)* miner (see [39]) is based on the Heuristics miner and therefore inherits its shortcomings (see [87, p. 232]). As the focus of this thesis is not on mining patterns in processes, the *Workflow patterns miner*(see [38]) is not taken into account.

## Conclusion

This *narrows the scope* of algorithms that can be used *in practice*. As a matter of fact, every other mining algorithm has known weaknesses and the *Fuzzy miner* is implemented in every discussed process mining tool, therefore it is brought to a *closer examination* in section 3.3.6.

### 3.3.6. Fuzzy Miner

The operation of the Fuzzy miner is described in the paper of Günther and van der Aalst ([41]). The Fuzzy miner does not search for patterns, but mines a "non-simplified" process model containing each and every activity and transition ever occurring in the log, without caring about significance in this first operation.

The next three steps aim to simplify the model:

**Conflict resolution**   is necessary, when two activities are connected in both directions, as this could be caused by a *loop of size two*, an *exception* or *concurrency* in the observed behavior (see [41, p. 337]). The conflict resolution and the underlying decisions can be influenced by the user via enabling or disabling the concurrency filter, or if enabled by adjusting the *preserve ratio* and the *ratio threshold* described in [41, pp. 337-338].

**Edge filtering**   is the second step to simplify the model. The Fuzzy miner contains an algorithm based on the significance and the correlation of transitions to extract the most relevant sequences of a process. While the *edge cutoff* parameter describes the overall aggressiveness of the algorithm, the balance between significance and correlation is set by the *utility root* parameter (see [41, pp. 338-339] for details).

**Node aggregation and abstraction**   According to [41, pp. 339-341] node aggregation and abstraction aims to preserve highly correlated groups of less-significant activities as aggregated clusters, while isolated less-significant activities are removed. Via the *node cutoff* parameter one can set a threshold, defining which activities become a *victim* to aggregation of abstraction, based on their significance.

**Discussion**

Adjusting the parameters of the filters is a crucial part for mining the control flow of a process, or in this case a network protocol. Infrequent behavior could be abstracted or aggregated, although it is functionally highly relevant to the network protocol. Empirical research and experience will lead to proper process models as the settings also depend on the underlying questions to answer. Abstraction helps to gain an overview of the process, but excessive abstraction or aggregation makes it impossible to gain correct conclusions.

Although Disco is based on the same mining algorithm, it offers only two parameters to adjust, the *Activities* and the *Path* parameter. It must therefore be concluded, that the behavior during conflict resolution cannot be influenced in Disco.

## 3.4. Process models

There are several notations for processes but the resulting model always has to fulfill the same quality criteria. The four quality dimensions worked on in [78, pp. 150] are fitness,simplicity, precision and generalization.

**Fitness**  is the ability of a model to replay a log. All variants of a process contained in the log are allowed by the model.

**Simplicity**  reflects the *keep it as simple as possible*-dictum. The easiest model explaining the behavior in the log is the best.

**Generalization**  is the key to *not overfitting* the log. Not each variant in the log should result in an extension of the model. Especially loops and concurrency could lead to an explosion of the process model as described in section 3.3.3.

**Precision**  is the key to *not underfitting* the log. The model has to be precise enough to avoid variants not seen in the log.

### Discussion

The quality dimensions are competing in some ways and have to be balanced by the mining algorithm. The *flower model*[78, p. 152] has perfect fitness and simplicity and allow any log to be replayed. The activities are *fully meshed* and allows any sequence of activities and the process is also generalized. On the other hand the model has poor precision as every sequence is allowed by the model, even those, not seen in the log. The *enumerating* model is the exact opposite, as there are sequential process fragments for any sequence observed and no other variants are allowed.

Mining algorithms like the *Fuzzy miner* allow to influence these criteria, as described in section 3.3.2, to shift the balance in any direction.

## 3.5. Findings - The weapons of choice

Disco is used for the first attempts in chapter 5 as it is "optimized for speed"[55]. As the tool does not provide the possibility to export the model (e.g. as a PNML file) for further processing, the RapidProM plugin for Rapidminer and/or ProM will be used for possible further examinations.

The narrow scope of algorithm implementations (see section 3.3.5), the findings from section 3.3.4 and the ability to convert Fuzzy nets into other notations lead the way to using the *Fuzzy miner*.

# 4. Prerequisites and -processing

This chapter leads the path from the capturing of network traffic up to the point, where the data is ready for process mining. The first step in this procedure is the ETL - extract, transform and load - process[78, p. 97] shown in figure 4.1.

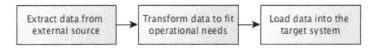

Figure 4.1.: Extract, transform, load

To narrow the scope, the event data needs to be filtered and fitted so that it contains only the data that is relevant for e.g. the TCP and is ready to be processed by process mining tools. This results in a gap between the *network world* and the *process mining world* as shown in table 4.1.

|  | Network Traffic | Gap | Process Mining |
|---|---|---|---|
| Tool | tshark | ← operation → | ProM |
| File Format | libpcap | ← syntactic → | XES |
| Information | Packet Headers, Payload | ← semantic → | Case ID, Event ID, Activity |
| additional Information | Packet Headers, Payload | ← semantic → | optional attributes |

Table 4.1.: Gap between network traffic and process mining

The following sections explore how this gap is bridged to allow proper process mining.

## 4.1. Data extraction

In this context *data extraction* means capturing network traffic. This is done with the tool *tshark*. Appendix B.9 describes the installation of tshark and gives some basic information on using this network package analyzer. Tshark offers many features for capturing, analyzing and transforming network traffic, while capturing and converting network captures are the key features in the scope of this chapter.

### Capturing network traffic

Before capturing network traffic, one needs to decide which network interfaces has to be listened to. Listing 4.1 shows how to display the available network interfaces.

```
~ tshark -D
1. en0 (Wi-Fi)
2. bridge0 (Thunderbolt Bridge)
3. awdl0
4. en1 (Thunderbolt 1)
5. p2p0
6. lo0 (Loopback)
```

Listing 4.1: List network interfaces with tshark

To capture network traffic, tshark is used like shown in listing 4.2. Tshark will capture the network traffic handled by the Wi-Fi network interface, until the desired size of 1Gigabyte (GB) is reached and save the result to the pointed file.

```
tshark -i Wi-Fi -a filesize:1000000 -w tshark.pcap
```

Listing 4.2: Capturing network traffic with tshark

Other variants of using tshark are mentioned in the user guide[32].

## 4.2. Data transformation

With *Wireshark* a closer look into each network packet can be taken to visualize further information. Information about the installation and usage of Wireshark can be found in Appendix B.10.

The packet headers hold all the information that is needed. A screenshot of Wireshark is shown in figure 4.2. All relevant information is marked with a red dot.

The *epoch time*, as part of the frame header, will be used as a timestamp for the event to make sure the correct chronological order of events. Alternatively the *frame number* could be considered as event ID. The combination of the *IP address* and the *source port* of the packet form the *resource*. The *stream index*

```
▼ Frame 1: 62 bytes on wire (496 bits), 62 bytes captured (496 bits)
    Encapsulation type: Ethernet (1)
    Arrival Time: Jun 11, 2010 17:28:33.689513000 CEST
    [Time shift for this packet: 0.000000000 seconds]
  ● Epoch Time: 1276270113.689513000 seconds
    [Time delta from previous captured frame: 0.000000000 seconds]
    [Time delta from previous displayed frame: 0.000000000 seconds]
    [Time since reference or first frame: 0.000000000 seconds]
    Frame Number: 1
    Frame Length: 62 bytes (496 bits)
    Capture Length: 62 bytes (496 bits)
    [Frame is marked: False]
    [Frame is ignored: False]
    [Protocols in frame: eth:ethertype:ip:tcp]
  ▶ Ethernet II, Src: Ibm_bb:ce:a1 (00:11:25:bb:ce:a1), Dst: Alcatel-_87:f5:94 (00:e0:b1:87:f5:94)
  ▶ Internet Protocol Version ●Src: 192.168.1.102 (192.168.1.102), Dst: 4.71.173.89 (4.71.173.89)
  ▼ Transmission Control Protocol, Src Port: 2686 (2686), Dst Port: 80 (80), Seq: 0, Len: 0
    ● Source Port: 2686 (2686)
      Destination Port: 80 (80)
    ● [Stream index: 0]
      [TCP Segment Len: 0]
      Sequence number: 0    (relative sequence number)
      Acknowledgment number: 0
      Header Length: 28 bytes
    ● .... 0000 0000 0010 = Flags: 0x002 (SYN)
      Window size value: 16384
      [Calculated window size: 16384]
    ▶ Checksum: 0x394b [validation disabled]
      Urgent pointer: 0
    ▶ Options: (8 bytes), Maximum segment size, No-Operation (NOP), No-Operation (NOP), SACK permitted
```

Figure 4.2.: TCP headers in Wireshark

is used as *case* or *trace ID*, while the *TCP flag* equates the *activity*. This leads to the mapping between the *network-* and the *process mining*-world as shown in table 4.2.

| Network packet header | → | Process mining |
|---|---|---|
| Epoch Time | → | Timestamp |
| Source IP and Source port | → | Resource |
| Stream index | → | Case/Trace ID |
| TCP flag | → | Activity |

Table 4.2.: Transformation of packet information

For elaborating on any other protocol the mapping has to be adapted to meet the requirements.

## From PCAP to PDML

In order to make the information, in the binary Packet CAPture (PCAP) file, human readable and easier to process with a scripting language it will be transformed into Packet Details Markup Language (PDML) (specification see [77]). PDML provides a detailed view of the packet's most important information related to the protocols and the fields found in the packet. The tool "tshark" is able to do this conversion. Appendix B.9 provides more information about tshark.

For the purposes of this thesis the PCAP file is converted with the command shown in listing 4.3. For the objective of filtering out a certain TCP stream a display filter has to be set as shown in listing 4.4.

```
tshark -r INPUT.pcap -T pdml >> OUTPUT.pdml
```

Listing 4.3: Conversion to PDML format with tshark

```
tshark -r INPUT.pcap -T pdml -Y "tcp.stream==0" >> OUTPUT.pdml
```

Listing 4.4: Conversion of certain TCP stream (0) to PDML format with tshark

The result of the conversion is the XML based file OUTPUT.pdml. The information found with Wireshark is stored in the XML structure as shown in listing 4.5.

```
<?xml version="1.0"?>
<?xml-stylesheet type="text/xsl" href="pdml2html.xsl"?>
<pdml version="0" creator="wireshark/1.99.5" time="Mon Jun 22 14
    :33:25 2015" capture_file="/Users/matthias/Desktop/train/test_
    all_pcm.pcap.TCP_4-73-173-89_60_192-168-1-102_2586.pcap">
<packet>
  <proto name="geninfo" pos="0" showname="General information" size="
      62">
    <field name="num" pos="0" show="1" showname="Number" value="1"
        size="62"/>
    <field name="len" pos="0" show="62" showname="Frame Length" value
        ="62" size="62"/>
    <field name="caplen" pos="0" show="62" showname="Captured Length"
        value="62" size="62"/>
    <field name="timestamp" pos="0" show="Jun 21, 2010 17:23:33
        .689513000 CEST" showname="Captured Time" value="
        1276270113.689513000" size="62"/>
  </proto>
```

```
<proto name="       " showname="
            size="  " pos=" ">
  ...
  <field name="           " showname="
                             " size="  " pos="  " show="
                    "/>
  ...
</proto>
<proto name="    " showname="
                             "
     size="   " pos="  ">
  ...
</proto>


<proto name="    " showname="
                             "
     size="   " pos="   ">
  ...
  <field name="       " showname="
                " size="  " pos="   " show="              " value=
          "/>
  ...
</proto>


<proto name="     " showname="
                             " size="  "
   pos="   ">
  ...
  <field name="        " showname="
              " size="  " pos="   " show="            " value="  "
     unmaskedvalue="     ">
  ...
  </field>
```

```
    ...
  </proto>
</packet>


<packet>

...

</packet>

...

</pdml>
```

Listing 4.5: Exemplary extract of a PDML file

The advantage of the XML based format is, that every part can be addressed via XML Path Language (XPath) when the entire ETL procedure is automated. All information highlighted in figure 4.2 is reflected in the resulting PDML file.

## Problem with incomplete TCP connections in Log

In section 3.1 the necessary quality of event data for process mining was explained in theory. When network traffic is captured one cannot be sure, that there are only complete (TCP-) sessions within the captured period of time. Figure 4.2 visualizes the problem.

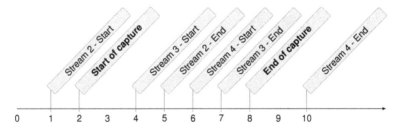

Figure 4.3.: chronology of events

The example in figure 4.2 shows, that there are several *incomplete processes* in this capture. This reflects real life situations where one can not be certain, that neither at the start nor at the end of the captured time frame noTCP sessions are open. Stream 2 started before the captured time frame. This means that the start of this process is not included in the event data and cannot be seen by the process mining algorithm. While TCP stream 3 is completely included in the event data, TCP stream 4 shows another problem. The end of the stream is not captured. Another possible variation is when the start and end of a

TCP stream are outside the captured time span. Given that it is impossible to capture only complete TCP sessions, this needs to be considered before mining the process. The process mining algorithm is not able to distinguish between complete and incomplete executions of a process. This situation will make the algorithm *detect* multiple start and end activities that do not represent reality.

This issue will be solved later on by filtering for certain start and end activities as shown in chapter 4.4.

**Distinguishing between server and client**

TCP controls the communication between a server and a client and the information about who sent which TCP flag is relevant. For the scope of this thesis the flags sent from the server to the client will be marked with a leading $x$.

For the HTTP protocol this information is not important, as the client sends a request[26, pp. 24-26] consisting of a predefined set of allowed methods[26, pp. 33-37] and the server has to respond[26, pp. 26-28] with a predefined set of status codes[26, pp. 37-45] and a message body if appropriate.

## 4.3. Load data

For the step of loading the data into the target system the PDML file needs further processing. The target system is a XES stored in a text file. The extracted and transformed event data has to be stored as a XES as described in section 3.1.2 which leads to a notation shown in listing 4.6.

```
<?xml version="1.0" encoding="UTF-8" ?>
<log xes.version="1.0" xmlns="http://www.xes-standard.org" xes.
   creator="Matthias Leeb">
   <extension name="Concept" prefix="concept" uri="http://www.xes-
      standard.org/concept.xesext"/>
   <extension name="Lifecycle" prefix="lifecycle" uri="http://www.xes-
      standard.org/lifecycle.xesext"/>
   <extension name="Time" prefix="time" uri="http://www.xes-standard.
      org/time.xesext"/>
   <extension name="Organizational" prefix="org" uri="http://www.xes-
      standard.org/org.xesext"/>
   <global scope="trace">
      <string key="concept:name" value="name"/>
```

```
</global>
<global scope="event">
  <string key="concept:name" value="name"/>
  <string key="lifecycle:transition" value="transition"/>
  <string key="org:resource" value="resource"/>
  <date key="time:timestamp" value="2011-04-13T14:02:31.197+02:00"/
    >
  <string key="Activity" value="string"/>
  <string key="Resource" value="string"/>
  <string key="concept:name" value="string"/>
  <string key="org:resource" value="string"/>
</global>
<classifier name="Activity" keys="concept:name"/>
<classifier name="Resource" keys="org:resource"/>
<string key="lifecycle:model" value="standard"/>
<string key="creator" value="Matthias Leeb"/>
<trace>
  <string key="concept:name" value="Stream_1"/>
  <event>
    <string key="lifecycle:transition" value="complete"/>
    <string key="concept:name" value="SYN"/>
    <string key="Activity" value="SYN"/>
    <string key="org:resource" value="10.0.1.3:58309"/>
    <date key="time:timestamp" value="2015-05-05T15:34:11.393+00:00
      "/>
    <string key="Resource" value="10.0.1.3:58309"/>
  </event>
  <event>
    <string key="lifecycle:transition" value="complete"/>
    <string key="concept:name" value="SYN,_ACK"/>
    <string key="Activity" value="SYN,_ACK"/>
    <string key="org:resource" value="109.75.181.14:80"/>
```

```
      <date key="time:timestamp" value="2015-05-05T15:34:11.417+05:00
      "/>
      <string key="Resource" value="109.75.191.24:80"/>
   </event>
   <event>
      <string key="lifecycle:transition" value="complete"/>
      <string key="concept:name" value="ACK"/>
      <string key="Activity" value="ACK"/>
      <string key="org:resource" value="10.0.1.3:58309"/>
      <date key="time:timestamp" value="2015-05-05T15:34:11.417+00:00
      "/>
      <string key="Resource" value="10.0.1.3:58309"/>
   </event>
...


...

   <event>
      <string key="lifecycle:transition" value="complete"/>
      <string key="concept:name" value="FIN,_ACK"/>
      <string key="Activity" value="FIN,_ACK"/>
      <string key="org:resource" value="10.0.1.3:58303"/>
      <date key="time:timestamp" value="2015-05-05T15:34:41.373+00:00
      "/>
      <string key="Resource" value="10.0.1.3:58303"/>
   </event>
   <event>
      <string key="lifecycle:transition" value="complete"/>
      <string key="concept:name" value="xACK"/>
      <string key="Activity" value="xACK"/>
      <string key="org:resource" value="109.75.191.24:80"/>
      <date key="time:timestamp" value="2015-05-05T15:34:41.405+00:00
      "/>
      <string key="Resource" value="109.75.191.24:80"/>
```

```
    </event>
  </trace>
</log>
```

Listing 4.6: Exemplary extract of the XES

The listing 4.6 shows three essential sections of the XES. In the log section some basic definitions take place and the structure of the following traces and events is defined. In the trace section a certain TCP stream is listed. The trace consists of man event sections that hold the information about a particular network packet. The first snippet of TCP stream 2 shows how the connection is established and the second snippet shows the closing. The extracted event data shows that the establishing and closing of the connection did meet the standard[63, pp. 30.31][63, pp. 37-39].

## 4.4. Automating the ETL procedure for TCP

In order to accelerate and automate the ETL procedure described in sections 4.1, 4.2 and 4.3 a script was developed. The sequence diagram (see figure 4.4) outlines the steps performed by the script.

The script is called with the PCAP file to process as a parameter. In a first step the amount of different TCP streams is determined. Only complete TCP streams should be taken into account. For this reason TCP streams without a SYN and a FIN or a RST flag will be filtered out. Each of the remaining streams is transformed into separate PDML files. Then a XES header is written to the XES file. For each stream, contained by a PDML file, a header, all events and a footer is appended to the XES file. After appending the XES footer, the resulting XES file is utilizable by a process mining tool (e.g. ProM or Disco).

The script is written in *Ruby* language. Additional information about Ruby can be found in appendix B.7.

## 4.5. Findings

The ETL process is a non-trivial and time consuming task. A deep understanding of the domain under observation is necessary for success.

The extraction of data assumes knowledge about computer networks to find the correct point in the network for tapping the traffic. This is even more relevant when dealing with virtualized or unfamiliar infrastructures.

The transformation of data and the loading of the same into the target system is a mixed up process in this domain. After converting the PCAP to a PDML file, all incomplete and non-TCP sessions are filtered.

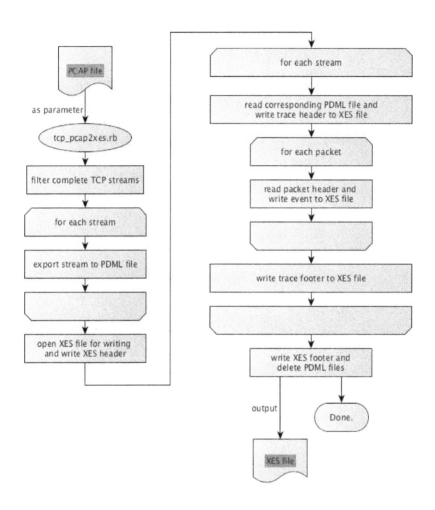

Figure 4.4.: pcap2xes for TCP

in another step only packets containing TCP headers are processed and written to the resulting XES.

# 5. Proof of Concept

In chapter 4 all basic steps were taken to start process mining. In this chapter the gained XES file is elaborated with the process mining tool *Disco*. Information about Disco can be found in appendix B.1. A conclusion regarding the application of control-flow discovery to network protocol TCP is derived from the lessons learned.

## 5.1. Mining TCP with Disco

The ETL process is applied to the network capture described in appendix A.2.1. The network capture contains the network traffic of a personal computer that is used for daily work.

### 5.1.1. Extracting relevant information

Extracting the relevant information and proper session information is achieved by the significant code snippets in listing 5.1 (extract of appendix C.1).

```
...
# extract TCP streams containing a SYN or a FIN or a RST flag
syn_streams = `tshark -r #{in_filename} -T fields -e tcp.stream 'tcp.
    flags == 0x0002' | sort -n | uniq`.split("\n")
finack_streams = `tshark -r #{in_filename} -T fields -e tcp.stream '
    tcp.flags == 0x0011' | sort -n | uniq`.split("\n")
rst_streams = `tshark -r #{in_filename} -T fields -e tcp.stream 'tcp.
    flags == 0x0004' | sort -n | uniq`.split("\n")

# Filter out streams that contain the SYN flag AND a (FIN/ACK OR RST)
    flag
streams = syn_streams & ( finack_streams || rst_streams )
```

```
...
# extract activity
        h_activity = packet.xpath(' proto[@name="tcp"]/field[@name="
                tcp.flags"]/@showname' ).to_s
...
packets.each do |packet|
        # Check if packet is part of a TCP connection
        if packet.to_s.include? "Transmission_Control_Protocol"
...
```

Listing 5.1: Filters for TCP

In the first snippet all complete TCP streams are filtered. This was accomplished by searching streams with a SYNor a FIN/ACK or a RST flag. With the boolean expression

$$streams = syn\_streams \land (finack\_streams \lor rst\_streams)$$

all streams, containing the FIN, ACK or RST flag and additionally contain the SYN flag are extracted. The second snippet shows how the activity - in this case the TCP flag - is extracted from the PDML file. The third snippet ensures, that only packets containing a TCP header - and therefore represent parts of the TCP communication - are left for further processing.

### 5.1.2. Results

#### Statistics

Disco can provide an overview of the TCP streams or cases. Information about the event data is summarized in the statistics tab of Disco.

Table 5.1 shows, that there are 6060 events in the event log. These events are spread over 167 cases in 113 variants. All cases can be composed with a set of 13 activities.

#### Activities and occurrence

Figure 5.1 shows the relative and absolute occurrence of activities. Activities performed by the client are left original and the ones performed by the server are marked with a leading $x$.

| Key | Value |
|---|---|
| Events | 6060 |
| Cases | 167 |
| Activities | 13 |
| Variants | 113 |

Table 5.1.: TCP: Basic stats of the event log

| Activity | Frequency | Relative frequency | |
|---|---|---|---|
| xACK | 2276 | 37.56 % | |
| ACK | 2022 | 33.37 % | |
| xPSH, ACK | 598 | 9.87 % | |
| PSH, ACK | 446 | 7.36 % | |
| FIN, ACK | 187 | 3.09 % | |
| xSYN, ACK | 182 | 3 % | |
| SYN | 167 | 2.76 % | |
| xFIN, ACK | 164 | 2.71 % | |
| RST | 14 | 0.23 % | |
| xFIN, PSH, ACK | 1 | 0.02 % | |
| xRST, ACK | 1 | 0.02 % | |
| xRST | 1 | 0.02 % | |
| RST, ACK | 1 | 0.02 % | |

Figure 5.1.: TCP Activities and their occurrence

**Process model**

Figure 5.2 shows the output of Disco containing the process model of the TCP, based on the captured behavior. Both the *activities* and the *paths* control (see section 3.3.6 for details) have been set to 100% to avoid aggregation or abstraction.

## 5.2. Discussion

The mined model is matched against the TCP standard[63] and the description of TCP in [74] based on the following leading questions:

1. Are there any non-standard flags?

2. Are the basic sequences during establishing and closing a session correctly represented by the model?

3. What are the limitations of the control-flow perspective?

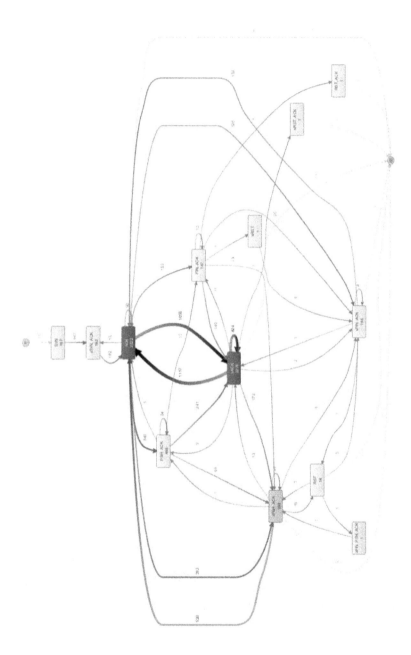

Figure 5.2.: TCP process model discovered by Disco

## 5.2.1. Recorded activities

All activities consist of one ore more of the flags SYN, ACK, PSH, RST and FIN. As the standard allows setting multiple flags within a network packet, all of these flags and their combinations are valid. Following the standard the URG flag is not recorded, which indicates, that the log is - as expected - incomplete as it can not contain any behavior defined in the standard.

## 5.2.2. Sequences

**Establishing a TCP session**    The standard defines the *three-way handshake* as an opening sequence for a TCP connection. Figure 5.3 - a section of figure 5.2 - reflects the simplest three-way handshake defined in [63, p.31]. All observed cases reflect this opening sequence.

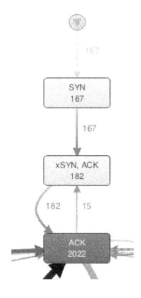

Figure 5.3.: Establish TCP connection

Following the standard, there are other possibilities to establish a connection (see [63, pp. 32]) that are not reflected by the model, again resulting from the incomplete log.

**Closing a TCP session**    For providing better overview a filter is applied:

- Only sessions ending with xACK (Acknowledge sent by server)

• Only sessions containing the "normal close sequence"[63, p. 39]

Figure 5.4 shows the result of this filter. This closing sequence - marked with red dots at the exit point

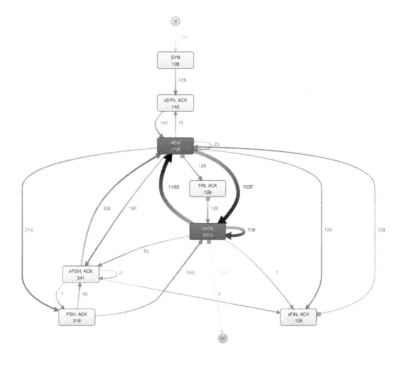

Figure 5.4.: Close TCP session

of each associated activity flowing from *xFIN, ACK* to *ACK* to *FIN, ACK* to *xACK* - is observed in 128 of all 167 cases.

### 5.2.3. Limitations

**ACK** The ACK flag is one of the six *control flags* defined in TCP. The ACK flag is set in the packet header and the *acknowledgement number* holds the expected sequence number to the corresponding packet sent earlier (see [63, p. 16]). In many cases the ACK flag is combined with other flags, allowing the communication to proceed with data transmission without sending two packets. This leads to several *combined or mixed* activities (SYN/ACK, FIN/ACK, and others). The ambiguous usage of ACK and other flags, complicates the mining of the original functional behavior of the protocol.

**States**   TCP is a *stateful protocol*, meaning that each activity causes a state transition as described in figure 5.5.

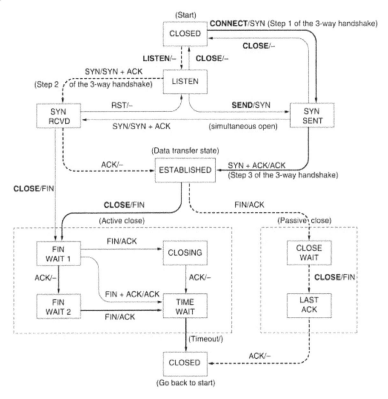

Figure 5.5.: TCP protocol(from [74])

The process visualization of Disco does not know *states* or *places* and the packet headers do not contain information about the state reached after a certain activity, so this information cannot be derived.

**Incompleteness**   To achieve a more comprehensive model and hence better knowledge of the control flow of TCP, a bigger capture of network traffic with more diversity regarding client computers is necessary.

## 5.3. Mining TCP with RapidMiner

To facilitate direct comparisons, the exact same network capture is investigated with RapidMiner and the RapidProM extension (ProM framework extension). Figure 5.6 shows the structure for this intention. The purpose of the function blocks is described left to right:

- ProM Context: Most of the ProM operators need a ProM context. This operator starts a ProM instance when executed.

- Multiply: The Multiply operator distributes the ProM context to every operator that needs one.

- Read Log: The Read Log operator imports the XES file for further processing. The file has to be configured in the parameter pane in RapidMiner.

- Add Artificial Start and End Event: Every case in the configured XES file gets a leading start and a trailing end event to provide better readability for the process model and ease the comparison to the model mined with Disco.

- Fuzzy Miner (Fuzzy Model): At the end of the structure the model is mined with this operator (see figure 5.7.

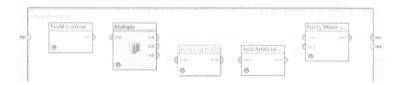

Figure 5.6.: RapidMiner: Mining process

Appendix A.4 holds the structure in figure 5.6 in XML format for easier reproduction. Only the path to the investigated XES file has to be adapted.

### 5.3.1. Adjustments in the results perspective

Many settings, that influence the resulting process model, can be adapted when using the Fuzzy Miner. *Concurrency*, *Edge* and *Node* filters can be adjusted. Section 3.3.6 explains the impact of these filters. As with Disco (see section 5.1), the controllers were set in a way to avoid aggregation or abstraction. The following paragraphs show how the filters have to be set to mine the control flow of the TCP shown in figure 5.7.

**Concurrency filter settings**

- Filter concurrency = TRUE

- Preserve = 0.000

- Ratio = 1.000

**Edge filter settings**  Settings in the edge filter tab:

- Fuzzy edges = TRUE

- Cutoff = 1.000

- Utility rt. = 0.000

- ignore self-loops = TRUE

- interpret absolute = FALSE

**Node filter settings**  Settings in the node filter tab:

- Significance cutoff = 0.000

**Discussion**

The process models mined by Disco (see figure 5.2) and Rapidminer (see 5.7) are identical due to their activities and the transitions between them. The tools deliver the same result when using the Fuzzy miner.

## 5.4. Findings

The proof of concept shows, that the previously introduced ETL procedure is correct. The mined process model eases the comparison of observed behavior to the TCP standard[63] and fundamental sequences of the control flow can be extracted.

The commercial tool Disco and the freeware RapidMiner with its RapidProM extension both deliver the exact same results. Disco delivers better visualization and statistics while RapidMiner provides more flexibility, especially on exporting the model for further processing.

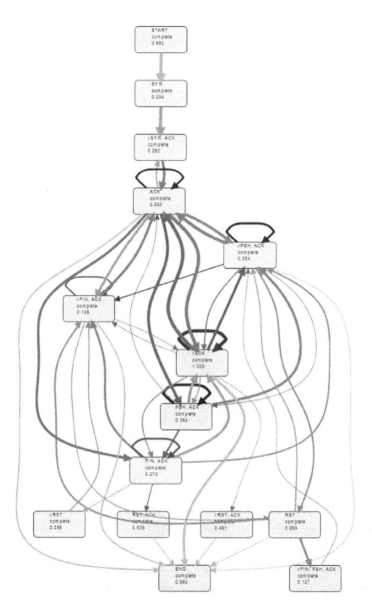

Figure 5.7.: RapidMiner: TCP process model

# 6. Reasonable applications, adaptions and enhancements

The following chapter examines other reasonable applications of process mining to network protocols. When dealing with other protocols than TCP or trying to work with big network captures (several Gigabytes size) the ETL process needs adaption or improvement. A suggestion for adaptions to the ETL process is given. An approach to predict, when observing more behavior does not significantly improve the model any more, is within the scope of this chapter.

## 6.1. Mining HTTP

In opposition to the stateful TCP this section concentrates on the *stateless HTTP*. The ETL process is applied to the network capture described in appendix A.2.2. The capture contains the network traffic of a computer, used to navigate through a newspapers website.

The structure of the ETL script for HTTP is all the same as it is with TCP. The filtering during the ETL script for HTTP is adapted to the different point of interest. Listing 6.1 shows the decisive snippets.

```
...
# extract TCP streams from pcap
streams = `tshark -r #{in_filename} -T fields -e tcp.stream | sort -n
    | uniq`.split("\n")

...

if doc.to_s.include? "Hypertext Transfer Protocol"

...

# extract activity
        activity = packet.xpath('proto[@name="http"]/field[1]/@show'
            ).to_s.chomp(" \r\n").upcase

...
```

```
# if activity is GET or POST cut off information
    if (activity.include?("GET") || activity.include?("POST"))
...
```

Listing 6.1: Filters for HTTP

The first snippet shows the filtering of all TCP streams to get rid of the User Datagram Protocol (UDP) packets. Only packets that contain a HTTP header are left after the filter in snippet two. The activity information resides at another section of the PDML file so the *xpath* has to be adapted as shown in snippet three. As each HTTP request is followed by the target path, which would lead to an activity for each subsite of a website, the target path is cut off to take only the request method as activity.

## 6.1.1. Results

### Statistics

Information about the event data is summarized in the statistics tab of Disco.

| Key | Value |
| --- | --- |
| Events | 1149 |
| Cases | 86 |
| Activities | 7 |
| Variants | 20 |

Table 6.1.: HTTP: Basic stats of the event log

Table 6.1 shows, that there are 1149 events in the event log. These events are spread over 86 cases in 20 variants. All cases can be composed of a set of 7 activities.

### Activities and occurrence

Figure 6.1 shows the relative and absolute occurrence of activities.

### Process model

Figure 6.2 shows the output of Disco containing the process model of HTTP, based on the captured behavior.

| Value | Δ Frequency | Relative frequency | |
|-------|-------------|--------------------|--|
| GET | 504 | 43.86 % | |
| HTTP/1.1 200 OK | 493 | 42.91 % | |
| HTTP/1.1 302 FOUND | 78 | 6.79 % | |
| [TRUNCATED]GET | 70 | 6.09 % | |
| POST | 2 | 0.17 % | |
| HTTP/1.1 304 NOT MODIFIED | 1 | 0.09 % | |
| HTTP/1.1 301 MOVED PERMANENTLY | 1 | 0.09 % | |

Figure 6.1.: HTTP: Activities and their occurrence

### 6.1.2. Discussion

The mined model is matched against the HTTP standard[26] based on the following leading questions:

1. Are there any non-standard requests or responses?

2. Are the basic sequences of requests and responses mined correctly?

3. What are the limitations of the control-flow perspective?

#### Recorded activities and sequences

According to the HTTP standard[26] the GET, $[TRUNCATED]$GET and the POST activities belong to the class of *request methods* sent by the client to request a certain resource, in case of a POST request, this is not obligatory as a HTTP/1.1 200 OK or other *responses* are also allowed. The responses observed in this log, including HTTP/1.1 200 OK, HTTP/1.1 302 FOUND, HTTP/1.1 304 NOT MODIFIED and HTTP/1.1 301 PERMANENTLY MOVED, are according to the standard. The log does not contain any deviations to the standard, as the principle of answering a request with a response in never broken.

#### Limitations

As might be expected, the model does not contain all possible request methods(see [26, p. 24]) and responses (see status codes in [26, p. 27]) due to incompleteness of the log.

## 6.2. Moving towards bigger captures

During development, the ETL script introduced in section 4.4 was continuously applied to smaller captures (self-captured, with a few Megabyte (MB) of size) finishing in an acceptable runtime. When using the network capture provided by the University of New Brunswick (see A.3 for details), some limitations showed up.

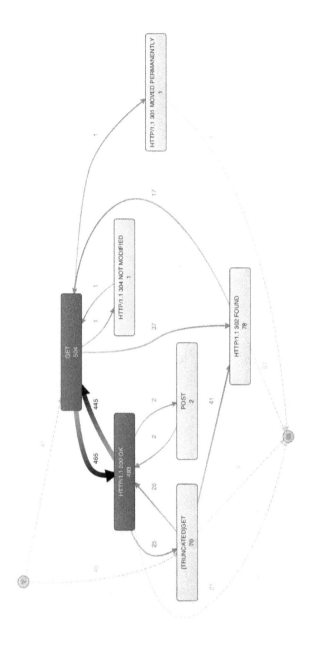

Figure 6.2.: HTTP process model discovered by Disco

As the PCAP file has to be processed the number of streams it contains plus one, the processing time sprawled out unacceptably. The runtime is influenced by the number of streams and the size of the capture itself. The goal is - as before - to split the captures by TCP stream, but in one run. As there is no known tool for Linux - except the one from Davids[11] which is insufficient, one can only move to the Windows-based Tool *SplitCap*.

## 6.2.1. SplitCap

SplitCap (see appendix B.8 for details) promises to solve this problem. A test showed, that SplitCap can split the extracted capture testbed-11jun of 17GB size by TCP streams in a reasonable time span of about an hour on a Solid-State-Drive (SSD)-equipped Laptop, while this would take several days with the method introduced in section 4.4. Listing 6.2 shows the used command:

```
C:SplitCap.exe -r testbed-11jun\testbed-11jun.pcap -o pcaps
Splitting pcap file into seperate pcap files...
100%
Please wait while closing all file handles...
```

Listing 6.2: Filters for TCP

This results in 276.773 PCAP files, of which 217.901 contain TCP streams, while the others are UDP streams.

## 6.2.2. Adaptions to the ETL script

In order to deal with this new situation the tcp_pcap2xes script is adapted as shown in appendix C.3. Instead of a complete PCAP file as a parameter, the folder containing the split PCAP files is passed to the script. The script is now called as shown in listing 6.3. The script has to be executed from the directory, where the result.xes file should reside after completion.

```
./tcp_pcap2xesNEW.rb /folderContainingPcaps
```

Listing 6.3: Command to call tcp_pcap2xesNEW script

## 6.3. Protocol reverse engineering

Reverse engineering of a protocol is, as outlined in [9] and [56], a time-consuming, error-prone, tedious and mostly manual task. During the proof of concept in chapter 5 the well-known TCP was used. If there is no prior knowledge of the protocol and its messages tools like *Discoverer*[9] and *AutoFormat*[56] help to examine the format of messages and the location of relevant data (like case ids, activities, resources or timestamps) for process mining. Having identified this fundamental knowledge, one can turn to think about the amount of event data necessary to mine the control flow.

To reverse engineer the control-flow model of a network protocol the size of the training set is relevant. Provided, that there is no reference model or other prior knowledge, the grade of alignment of the model with the observed behavior has to be predicted in another way. The following considerations are based on the assumption, that the *information gain* per case, leading to enhancements of the process model decreases, when more and more cases are added to the log. In order to simulate a real-life situation, the log will be expanded with randomly chosen cases. The file testbed-11jun (from A.3) previously split with the tool SplitCap serves as a basis for this intention.

### 6.3.1. Gathering data

To create a random subset of the TCP streams observed in testbed-11jun the commands in listing 6.4 are used.

```
find . | perl -MList::Util=shuffle -e 'print shuffle <>' | head -n
   1000 > random1000.txt
for f in `cat random1000.txt` ; do mv $f /Users/matthias/Desktop/
   temp_pcap ; done
```

Listing 6.4: Getting 1000 random files from directory

The example shows, how a random subset of 1000 files in the current directory is moved to another directory. The first command lists all files in the current directory. A *perl* (see section B.2 for details) command shuffles the output and finally the first thousand entries are written to a text file. The second command moves every file listed in the previously generated text file to another directory.

This is done sequentially with an increasing number of cases and the average information gain (aig) is measured after 1, 2, 5, 10, 20, 50, 100, 200, 500 and 1000 cases. The methods introduced in section 5.1 and 6.2 are then applied to each subset. For each random subset the Information value (Iv) is calculated by summing up the number of activities and transitions.

## 6.3.2. Results

Table 6.2 presents the gathered data. The activities(a) and the transitions(t) between them are counted for each number of cases(c) and summed to the $Iv$ of each subset of cases:

$$Iv = a + t$$

The aig is calculated the following way:

$$aig = \frac{Iv}{c}$$

| Cases | Variants | Events | Activities | Transitions | Information value | avg. information gain |
|-------|----------|--------|------------|-------------|-------------------|------------------------|
| 1 | 1 | 1087 | 8 | 18 | 26 | 26.000 |
| 2 | 2 | 1097 | 8 | 19 | 27 | 13.500 |
| 5 | 5 | 1575 | 9 | 29 | 38 | 7.600 |
| 10 | 10 | 2264 | 10 | 33 | 43 | 4.300 |
| 20 | 17 | 3161 | 11 | 38 | 49 | 2.450 |
| 50 | 39 | 4447 | 11 | 40 | 51 | 1.020 |
| 100 | 72 | 9729 | 11 | 44 | 55 | 0.550 |
| 200 | 124 | 15516 | 13 | 54 | 67 | 0.335 |
| 500 | 303 | 37067 | 14 | 62 | 76 | 0.152 |
| 1000 | 560 | 78097 | 15 | 68 | 83 | 0.083 |

Table 6.2.: Statistics of TCP

Figure 6.3 shows the aig (blue crosses) and the trendline (red)

$$aig = 26.9652 * c^{-0.8323}$$

with a coefficient of determination

$$R^2 = 0.9988$$

.

**Trendline fitting**

To fit the trendline the tool *R* (see appendix B.4 for details) is used. To simplify the usage, the Graphical User Interface (GUI) *RStudio* (see appendix B.6 for details) is used. Listing 6.5 shows the performed calculations.

```
> aigOverCases <- read.csv("~/aig.txt")
>   View(aigOverCases)
> Base10 <- log10(aigOverCases)
> lm(aig ~ cases, data = Base10)

Call:
lm(formula = aig ~ cases)

Coefficients:
(Intercept)         cases
    1.4308       -0.8323

> summary(lm(aig ~ cases, Base10))

Call:
lm(formula = aig ~ cases, data = Base10)

Residuals:
      Min         1Q     Median         3Q        Max
-0.049926  -0.015587  -0.005401   0.026158   0.041197

Coefficients:
             Estimate Std. Error t value Pr(>|t|)
(Intercept)   1.43080    0.01821   78.57 7.67e-13 ***
cases        -0.83229    0.01022  -81.42 5.77e-13 ***
---
Signif. codes:  0 '***' 0.001 '**' 0.01 '*' 0.05 '.' 0.1 ' ' 1
```

```
Residual standard error: 0.03107 on 8 degrees of freedom
Multiple R-squared:  0.9988,    Adjusted R-squared:  0.9986
F-statistic:  6630 on 1 and 8 DF,  p-value: 5.772e-13
> a <- 10^(summary(lm(aig ~ cases, data = Base10))$coefficients[1,
    1])
> a
[1] 26.96521
> b <- summary(lm(aig ~ cases, data = Base10))$coefficients[2, 1]
> b
[1] -0.8322902
> R2 <- summary(lm(aig ~ cases, data = Base10))$r.squared
> R2
[1] 0.9987948
```

Listing 6.5: Trendline fitting with R

The first two lines show the loading of the dataset into RStudio. As the graph with measured aig with logarithmic scale (see figure 6.3) shows a nearly straight line, the complete dataset (cases and aig) is transformed (logarithmize aig and c) to be able to apply linear regression (lm). The coefficients of the equation

$$aig = a * c^b$$

are extracted and $a$ has to be transformed back (de-logarithmized) to step back to nonlinear regression, while b simply is taken as the exponent. This leads to the equation mentioned above. The coefficient of determination $R^2$ is extracted from the summary.

**Verification**

To verify the approach the procedure is repeated twice, leading to the data shown in table 6.3. The result is shown in table 6.4 and the corresponding figure 6.4.

### 6.3.3. Discussion

The activities and transitions reflect the information gain of cases due to the process model in the best possible way as they have direct impact. The amount of variations can not be used for this purpose as variations group process instances the show up the exact same sequence of activities. Thinking of loops, different numbers of repetitions lead to different variations, but this has no impact on the process model.

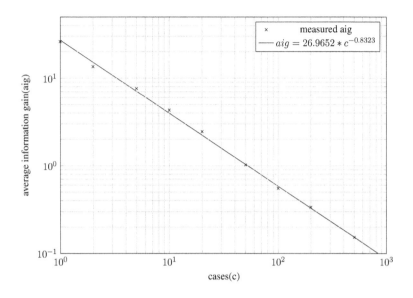

Figure 6.3.: Average information gain over number of cases

| Cases | Test 1 | | | | Test 2 | | | | Test 3 | | | |
|---|---|---|---|---|---|---|---|---|---|---|---|---|
| | Act. | Trans. | Iv | aig | Act. | Trans. | Iv | aig | Act. | Trans. | Iv | aig |
| 1 | 8 | 18 | 26 | 26.000 | 8 | 14 | 22 | 22.000 | 7 | 11 | 19 | 19.000 |
| 2 | 8 | 19 | 27 | 13.500 | 9 | 19 | 28 | 14.000 | 10 | 20 | 30 | 15.000 |
| 5 | 9 | 29 | 38 | 7.600 | 9 | 23 | 31 | 6.200 | 11 | 29 | 40 | 8.000 |
| 10 | 10 | 33 | 43 | 4.300 | 11 | 29 | 40 | 4.000 | 12 | 37 | 49 | 4.900 |
| 20 | 11 | 38 | 49 | 2.450 | 12 | 38 | 50 | 2.500 | 12 | 39 | 51 | 2.550 |
| 50 | 11 | 40 | 51 | 1.020 | 13 | 50 | 63 | 1.260 | 13 | 49 | 62 | 1.240 |
| 100 | 11 | 44 | 55 | 0.550 | 13 | 71 | 84 | 0.840 | 14 | 56 | 70 | 0.700 |
| 200 | 13 | 54 | 67 | 0.335 | 14 | 73 | 87 | 0.436 | 14 | 62 | 76 | 0.380 |
| 500 | 14 | 62 | 76 | 0.152 | 14 | 79 | 93 | 0.186 | 14 | 74 | 88 | 0.176 |
| 1000 | 15 | 68 | 83 | 0.083 | 14 | 85 | 99 | 0.099 | 14 | 87 | 101 | 0.101 |

Table 6.3.: Verifying first result

| Test | a | b | $R^2$ |
|------|---|---|-------|
| 1 | 26.9652108960633 | -0.832290241028435 | 0.9987948 |
| 2 | 23.5828089169813 | -0.767715230367619 | 0.9964178 |
| 3 | 25.2922547003560 | -0.787137799699707 | 0.9951289 |

Table 6.4.: Comparing resulting equations and coefficient of determination

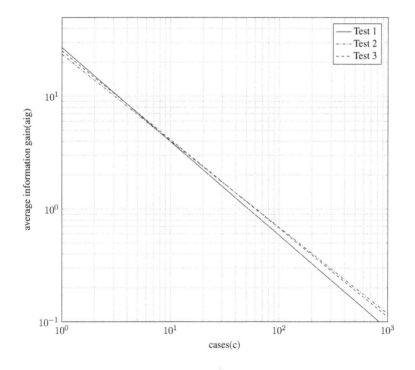

Figure 6.4.: Comparison of trendlines

Events are not meaningful for the same reason.

The comparison of the resulting trendlines show that test 1 results in a more optimistic estimation than the following tests 2 and 3. Coefficients of determination are close to one for all three tests.

The following assumptions show two possible use cases for this procedure.

**Assumption 1**  To discover a process, a big amount of log is available. Investigating the complete log is expensive and time consuming.

By applying the procedure and picking a random and increasing number of cases one can estimate the necessary size of the fraction of the log, which is sufficient to mine a proper process model.

**Assumption 2**  When doing process discovery the equation and its coefficient of determination could be computed after each added case. When the coefficient of determination reaches a predefined value, the number of cases that have to be observed to mine a proper process model can be estimated. This avoids spending too many resources on gathering logs on the one hand and shortens the ETL process on the other hand.

**Limitation**  In order to be in the position to fully verify the approach the procedure has to be repeated several hundred (or even thousand) times. This is not done within this thesis, as it requires automation and further examination.

## 6.4. Findings

For mining a different protocol, the ETL procedure has to be adapted in reply to the different objective. The mining results show the structure of a HTTP communication in detail and provide a correct reflection of the standard.

When dealing with network captures with a size of 1 GB and more, the ETL procedure has to be optimized due to save resources. This is accomplished by using the SplitCap tool, which is capable of splitting a network capture in one run, instead of sequentially.

Section 6.3 answers the question, how many instances of a process have to be observed, to mine a "good-enough" model. By introducing a metric based on the $lv$ of a case (sum of activities and transitions), the $aig$ gain is inspected over a rising number of cases and a trendline is derived. The number of cases, when inspecting even more of the does not result in a certain proportionate change of the process model, can be predicted.

# 7. Conclusion

This thesis was set out to explore the application of process mining to network protocols. Process mining is applied to (business) processes with the goal of discovering, enhancing or checking these processes for conformity. From the information security's point of view, these goals are worthwhile too. The fact that processes and protocols have things in common underlines this idea. As a matter of fact, additional help for reverse engineering or reengineering network protocols, check their conformity or investigating them for enhancement would be a welcome addition to or even a replacement for the contemporary practice of mostly manual, complex and error-prone analysis, based on fiction or feelings rather than facts in form of event data logged by today's information systems or observed network traffic.

Based on these ideas, the thesis sought to answer these research questions:

1. Which perspectives and types of process mining are significant to network protocols?

2. Which process mining algorithms and notation systems are viable?

3. What are the requirements and prerequisites to process captured network traffic with process mining tools?

4. What are reasonable applications of process mining in the field of network protocols?

**Results** If one looks at the BPM life-cycle, the feedback loop between (re)design (based on models) and observed reality (based on data) is a loose link. Process mining can close this feedback loop and support and trigger the BPM life-cycle, to overcome this limitation and short-circuit process models and event data.

Aspects and questions of a network protocol can be answered with process mining, if the correct combination of perspective and type is applied. The types *discovery*, *conformance* and *enhancement* crossed with the perspectives *control-flow*, *organization*, *case* and *time* or *frequencies*, to name but a few, allow the investigation of functional and technical aspects of a network protocol. While this thesis concentrates on the discovery of control-flow, other combinations allow for questions with a different focus.

To ensure high-quality results in process mining event data, mining algorithms and notation systems have to fulfill certain quality measures and have certain capabilities. The quality of event data is quantified as noise and incompleteness and the event data has to be well structured. The tools Disco and ProM prefer the event data in the XES format.

To reach optimal mining results, choosing the best possible combination of the process mining algorithm, the notation system and the process mining tool is of particular importance. When looking at problems with evaluating algorithms (section 3.3.1), the categorization of algorithms (section 3.3.4), the challenges for algorithms and notation systems (3.3.3) and the available implemented plug-ins for control-flow mining, the Fuzzy miner emerged as the algorithm of choice.

The notation system is a result of the chosen mining algorithm or plug-in and its output format, in this case a fuzzy net. Irrespective of this, conversion plug-ins between notation systems exist.

The process models have four underlying and often competing quality criteria - namely fitness, simplicity, generalization and precision - that have to be balanced according to the desired outcome. When mining for the control-flow of network protocols, any abstraction or aggregation has to be avoided as this means information loss due to rarer process sequences.

An ETL procedure is necessary to apply process mining to event data of information systems. In the domain of network protocols, this means capturing network data (*extraction*), converting it to a utilizable format (*transform*) and *load* it into the process mining tool. The extraction is performed with tshark resulting in a PCAP file. Tshark also converts the file into a XML-based PDML file that is transformed to a XES file. During this last transformation only relevant data , useful for the goal of mining the control-flow of the TCP protocol, is distilled.

Having completed the ETL procedure, first Disco, then RapidProM are used to mine the process model for TCP. Both tools, when adjusted correctly to avoid abstraction and aggregation, deliver the exact same process model. Basic sequences, like establishing and closing a TCP session are reflected correctly in the resulting models. The proof of concept can be assessed as successful.

Keeping the proof of concept in mind and turning to the HTTP protocol the ETL procedure needs adaption. The filters formerly used for picking the activities for the TCP protocols from the captured network traffic, were adapted for mining the HTTP, again resulting in a valid process model reflecting the HTTP standard.

To conserve resources when dealing with large network captures the ETL process was optimized. Using a more efficient tool to split network captures into separate TCP streams in one run - instead of one for each TCP stream - the ETL procedure for a network capture of 17GB size can be carried out on a customary SSD-equipped laptop within a time-span of two hours. Without this measure, the ETL procedure would consume several days.

Reverse engineering a network protocol based on big network captures of a few GB size is a resource and time consuming task. To clarify, whether enough event data is available or to estimate how many cases one has to observe or analyze, to mine a *good-enough* process model, a metric is introduced in section 6.3. A relation between added cases and their impact on the process model is measured and a derived trendline is rated by its coefficient of determination, leading to acceptable results. All three attempts with a randomly generated set of TCP streams, are leading to a coefficient of determination larger than 0.995 . This suggests the average information gain is decreasing along a certain trendline and one can stop observing a process, when a self defined minimum information gain threshold is crossed.

**Limitations and considerations**    While mining the TCP protocol, the combination of two or more activities leads to confusion. The ambiguous usage - used to confirm different preceding activities - and combined usage - confirming the last activity while sending a new one in the same process step (e.g. PSH and ACK flags set) - of the ACK flag adds complexity to the resulting model.

Also the ability of the fuzzy mining algorithm to abstract and aggregate activities has to be kept in mind, as this does not support the goal of mining the control flow and finding a model, that exactly represents the observed reality.

Process mining can be applied to network protocols delivering comprehensive insight, when the right perspectives are chosen and the ETL procedure is trimmed to extract the corresponding data. Another strength of process mining is the automated visualization of observed behavior, enabling discussion and further examination of network protocols.

**Outlook**    There is no doubt about the usability of process mining for network protocols. This thesis concentrates on control-flow mining of network protocols and there is room for further investigations:

- The gap between the world of network protocols and the process mining domain results in the necessity for adapting the ETL procedure for each and every protocol and perspective. If process mining tools could read network captures (e.g. the PCAP or PDML format) directly, this would make investigations much faster and easier.

- To fully investigate a network protocol, concentrating on the control flow is insufficient. Other additional perspectives have to be taken into account to completely understand a network protocol.

- To proof the effectiveness of process mining network protocols, a none or hardly documented or proprietary protocol is worth elaborating on. Also the validation of the average information gain metric and the resulting trendline needs professionalization and automation.

- In addition to the metric introduced in section 6.3, cross-validation of event data in itself and later on against a process model could be used to quantify the quality of both, the event data used for training and the derived process model.

**Essence**  The concept of process mining can be applied to network protocols and delivers useful results. The path adopted, from determining the best possible set of tools (algorithm and notation system) to developing and automating the ETL procedure and inferring a process model of the TCP, leads to satisfactory output. Adaptions to the ETL procedure delivered the possibility to mine the control flow of the HTTP and a performance boost, when dealing with big amounts of event data. A metric for estimating the average information gain over a growing number of cases was introduced, to derive a trendline.

# A. Data

## A.1. Example PNML file

The file example.pnml if found on the CD in the folder data\pnml and contains the exemplary Petri net used for illustration in section 2.4.1.

## A.2. Self-captured

### A.2.1. tcpCapture.pcap

The file tcpCapture.pcap is found on the DVD in the folder data\pcaps and contains a network capture of 4.8 MB size, recorded during every-day work on a private laptop.

### A.2.2. httpCapture.pcap

The file httpCapture.pcap is found on the DVD in the folder data\pcaps and contains network traffic captured during surfing a newspapers website.

## A.3. External

The University of New Brunswick in Canada [12] provides the *ISCX 2012 Intrusion Detection Evaluation Dataset*[13]. In the scope of this thesis the dataset is used for mining the TCP protocol and possibly others. The provided testbed-11jun.7z - or parts of it - is used for all analysis and examinations.

## A.4. RapidMiner structure

```
<?xml version="1.0" encoding="UTF-8" standalone="no"?>
<process version="5.3.015">
  <context>
    <input/>
```

```
<output/>
<macros/>
</context>
<operator activated="true" class="process" compatibility="5.3.015"
  expanded="true" name="Process">
  <process expanded="true">
    <operator activated="true" class="prom:prom_context"
      compatibility="2.0.002" expanded="true" height="60" name="
      ProM_Context" width="90" x="45" y="30"/>
    <operator activated="true" class="multiply" compatibility="
      5.3.015" expanded="true" height="94" name="Multiply" width="
      90" x="179" y="30"/>
    <operator activated="true" class="prom:read_log" compatibility=
      "2.0.002" expanded="true" height="60" name="Read_Log_(Path)"
      width="90" x="313" y="75">
      <parameter key="filename" value="/PATH/TO/repcapture.xes"/>
    </operator>
    <operator activated="true" class="
      prom:add_artificial_start_end_event_filter" compatibility="
      2.0.002" expanded="true" height="60" name="Add_Artificial_
      Start_and_End_Event" width="90" x="447" y="75"/>
    <operator activated="true" class="prom:mine_fuzzy_model"
      compatibility="2.0.002" expanded="true" height="76" name="
      Fuzzy_Miner_(Fuzzy_Model)" width="90" x="591" y="30"/>
    <connect from_op="ProM_Context" from_port="context_(ProM_
      Context)" to_op="Multiply" to_port="input"/>
    <connect from_op="Multiply" from_port="output_1" to_op="Fuzzy_
      Miner_(Fuzzy_Model)" to_port="context"/>
    <connect from_op="Multiply" from_port="output_2" to_op="Read_
      Log_(Path)" to_port="context_(ProM_Context)"/>
    <connect from_op="Read_Log_(Path)" from_port="event_log_(ProM_
      Event_Log)" to_op="Add_Artificial_Start_and_End_Event"
      to_port="event_log_(ProM_Event_Log)"/>
```

```
<connect from_op="                                   " from_port
    ="                                   " to_op="
             " to_port="             "/>
<connect from_op="                         " from_port="
                 " to_port="             "/>
<portSpacing port="                   " spacing="  "/>
<portSpacing port="                 " spacing="  "/>
<portSpacing port="                 " spacing="  "/>
    </process>
  </operator>
</process>
```

Listing A.1: RapidMiner structure

# B. Tools and software

*OS X Yosemite*[44] is used during this thesis so in default the instructions here only care about this operating system, otherwise this is mentioned as separate matter.

## B.1. Disco

Disco[55] is a commercial product of *Fluxicon Process Laboratories* for the purpose of process mining. A short tour[66], a comprehensive user guide[67] and installation instructions[68] are available. The license for this thesis was obtained via the *academic initiative*[1].

## B.2. Perl

"Perl 5 is a highly capable, feature-rich programming language with over 27 years of development."[60] Documentation is found on the website [61] and the software can be downloaded under [62]. The version used in this thesis is *perl5 (revision 5 version 18 subversion 2)*.

## B.3. ProM

"ProM is an extensible framework that supports a wide variety of process mining techniques in the form of plug-ins. It is platform independent as it is implemented in Java, and can be downloaded free of charge."[21] In the context of theis Thesis ProM is used for process mining. The Process Mining Group provides information[21], documentation[22] and a source for download[23].

## B.4. R

"R is a free software environment for statistical computing and graphics. It compiles and runs on a wide variety of UNIX platforms, Windows and MacOS."[28]

---

[1]http://fluxicon.com/academic/

Documentation is found on the website [29] and the software can be downloaded under [30]. The version used in this thesis is *3.2.1 (2015-06-18) – "World-Famous Astronaut"*.

## B.5. RapidMiner and RapidProM

RapidMiner is a tool for advanced analytics, predictive analytics, data mining, ETL and Reporting (extracted from [64]

Documentaion is found in the company website([65]). The tools can be downloaded from sourceforge(see [64]. The version 5.3.015 is used in the context of this thesis.

Extensions for RapidMiner - as in this case the RapidProM extension - enrich the features and possibilities. Documentation and install instructions for RapidProM are located at [75] and [76]. Version 2.0.2 is used in the context of this thesis

## B.6. RStudio

"RStudio IDE is a powerful and productive user interface for R. It's free and open source, and works great on Windows, Mac, and Linux."[71]

Documentation is found on the website [72] and the software can be downloaded under [73]. The version used in this thesis is *0.99.447.*

## B.7. Ruby

"Ruby is...

A dynamic, open source programming language with a focus on simplicity and productivity. It has an elegant syntax that is natural to read and easy to write."[8] Within the scope of this thesis the Ruby version 2.1.1 was used. The integrated development environment (IDE) *Rubymine*[47] from *JetBRAINS*[48] was used for development.

## B.8. SplitCap

*SplitCaps* website hold information and and a brief manual (see [3]). The tools can be downloaded from *sourceforge*(see [4]).

## B.9. tshark

*tshark* is shipped with the installation of Wireshark. Further information about the tool and the user guide can be found on the Wireshark website[32].

## B.10. Wireshark

Wireshark[33] is a network packet analyzer. Broadly they will apply to other operating systems too.

1. Download Wireshark Installer[34] fitting your operating system

2. Install Wireshark following the vendors instructions in the "Wireshark User's Guide"[35]

There are some OSX-specific limitations to the current development release of Wireshark (e.g. Wireshark 1.99.5). Not all features are available in comparison to the stable version provided, but no X server is required. As Wireshark is only used for manual packet inspection, feature completeness is not relevant in the context of this thesis.

## B.11. WoPeD

"WoPeD is an open-source software developed at the Cooperative State University Karlsruhe under the GNU Lesser General Public License (LGPL). The main goal is to provide an easy-to-use software for modelling, simulating and analyzing processes described by workflow nets, a Petri net class initially introduced by Wil van der Aalst (TU Eindhoven)."[36] The tool can be downloaded from the WoPeD website[37]

# C. Sourcecode

## C.1. Script tcp_pcap2xes.rb

```ruby
#!/usr/bin/env ruby


require 'rubygems'
require 'nokogiri'
require 'xml'
require 'time'
require 'date'
require 'ruby-progressbar'


# check number of arguments
if 1 != ARGV.size
  STDERR << "Usage: #{$0} in.pcap"
  exit(2)
end


# store arguments in variables
in_filename = ARGV[0]


p "Starting conversion of pcap..."


# extract TCP streams containing a SYN or a FIN or a RST flag
syn_streams = `tshark -r #{in_filename} -T fields -e tcp.stream 'tcp.
    flags == 0x0002' | sort -n | uniq`.split("\n")
finack_streams = `tshark -r #{in_filename} -T fields -e tcp.stream '
    tcp.flags == 0x0011' | sort -n | uniq`.split("\n")
```

```
rst_streams = 'tshark -r #{in_filename} -T fields -e tcp.stream 'tcp.
    flags == 0x0004' | sort -n | uniq'.split("\n")


# Filter out streams that contain the SYN flag AND a (FIN/ACK OR RST)
    flag
streams = syn_streams & ( finack_streams || rst_streams )


p streams.count.to_s + "_complete_TCP_streams_found."


# convert pcaps tp pdml separated by tcp.stream
p "Splitting...."
bar = ProgressBar.create(:total => streams.count)
streams.each do |stream|
    'tshark -r #{in_filename} -T pdml -Y "tcp.stream==#{stream.to_s}"
        >> pdml/#{in_filename}-#{stream.to_s}.pdml'
    bar.increment
end


p "Done."


# create XES file
open("pdml/#{in_filename}.xes", 'w') do |file|


    # write XES header
    file << "<?xml_version=\"1.0\"_encoding=\"UTF-8\"_?>\n"
    file << "<log_xes.version\"_.0\"_xmlns=\"https://www.xes-standard.
        org\"_xes.creator=\"Matthias_Leeb\">\n"


    file << "__<extension_name=\"Concept\"_prefix=\"concept\"_uri=\"
        http://www.xes-standard.org/concept.xesext\"/>\n"
    file << "__<extension_name=\"Lifecycle\"_prefix=\"lifecycle\"_uri
        =\"http://www.xes-standard.org/lifecycle.xesext\"/>\n"
```

```
file << "___<extension_name=\"Time\"_prefix=\"time\"_uri=\"http:
www.xes-standard.org/time.xesext\"/>\n"
file << "___<extension_name=\"Organizational\"_prefix=\"org\"_uri=\"
http://www.xes-standard.org/org.xesext\"/>\n"

file << "___<global_scope=\"trace\">\n"
file << "_____<string_key=\"concept:name\"_value=\"name\"/>\n"
file << "___</global>\n"

file << "___<global_scope=\"event\">\n"
file << "_____<string_key=\"concept:name\"_value=\"name\"/>\n"
file << "_____<string_key=\"lifecycle:transition\"_value=\"
transition\"/>\n"
file << "_____<string_key=\"org:resource\"_value=\"resource\"/>\n"
file << "_____<date_key=\"time:timestamp\"_value=\"2011-04-13T14
:02:31.199+02:00\"/>\n"
file << "_____<string_key=\"Activity\"_value=\"string\"/>\n"
file << "_____<string_key=\"Resource\"_value=\"string\"/>\n"
file << "_____<string_key=\"concept:name\"_value=\"string\"/>\n"
file << "_____<string_key=\"org:resource\"_value=\"string\"/>\n"
file << "___</global>\n"

file << "___<classifier_name=\"Activity\"_keys=\"concept:name\"/>\n"
    file << "___<classifier_name=\"Resource\"_keys=\"org:resource
\"/>\n"
    file << "___<string_key=\"lifecycle:model\"_value=\"standard
\"/>\n"
file << "___<string_key=\"creator\"_value=\"Matthias_Leeb\"/>\n"

number = 0
p "Start_writing_XES_..."
bar = ProgressBar.create(:total => streams.count)
streams.each do |trace|
```

```
number += 1
# begin trace
file << "  <trace> \n"
file << "  _ string_key=\"concept:name\"_value=\"Stream_" +
  trace.to_s + " \"/> \n"

# write events
doc = Nokogiri::XML(File.open("pdml/#/ip_filename}-#{trace.to_s}.
  pdml"))
packets = doc.xpath(' /pdml//packet')
pnumber = 0
initiator = ""

packets.each do |packet|
  # Check if packet is part of a TCP connection
  if packet.to_s.include? "Transmission_Control_Protocol"
    # count packets in stream          ,
    pnumber = pnumber + 1

    # extract relevant data via xpath
    # whos the actor/resource fo the current activity
    actor = packet.xpath(' proto[@name="ip"]/field[@name="ip.src
      "]/@show').to_s + ":" + packet.xpath(' proto[@name="tcp"]/
      field[@name="tcp.srcport"]/@show').to_s
    # packet/activity arrival time
    epoch = packet.xpath(' proto[@name="frame"]/field[@name="frame
      .time_epoch"]/@show').to_s
    # extract activity
    h_activity = packet.xpath(' proto[@name="tcp"]/field[@name="
      tcp.flags"]/@showname').to_s

    # remove unnecessary characters from TCP flag
```

```
activity = h_activity.slice(h_activity.index(' ')+1 ..
    h_activity.index(' ')-1)
# bring epoch time to format for XES
timestamp = DateTime.strptime(epoch.to_s, '  ').strftime('
    ').gsub(' ', (' % epoch).to_s
    .split(' ').last).to_s


# Who initiated the connection? -> Sender of first packet in
    stream
if pnumber < 2
    initiator = packet.xpath('
    ').to_s + "  " + packet.xpath('
    ').to_s
end


# write event
file << "
file << "
    
# distinguish between activities of the two actors by leading
    X
if actor.eql?(initiator)
    file << "
    activity + "
    file << "
    activity + "
else
    file << "
    activity + "
    file << "
    activity + "
end
```

```ruby
      file << "          <string_key=\"org:resource\"_value=\"" + actor
          + "\"/>\n"
      file << "          <date_key=\"time:timestamp\"_value=\"" +
          timestamp + "\"/>\n"
      file << "          <string_key=\"Resource\"_value=\"" + actor + "
          \"/>\n"

      file << "          </event>\n"
      # event closed
    end
  end
  # close trace
  file << "      </trace>\n"
  bar.increment
  end


  # write XES footer
  file << "</log>"
end


# Delete unnecessary pdml files
p "cleaning_up..."
`rm pdml/*.pdml`
p "DONE."
```

Listing C.1: tcp_pcap2xes.rb

## C.2. Script http_pcap2xes.rb

```ruby
#!/usr/bin/env ruby


require 'rubygems'
require 'nokogiri'
require 'xes'
require 'time'
```

```ruby
require 'date'
require 'ruby-progressbar'

# check number of arguments
if 1 != ARGV.size
  STDERR << "Usage: #{$0} in.pcap"
  exit(2)
end

# store arguments in variables
in_filename = ARGV[0]

p "Starting conversion of pcap..."

# extract TCP streams from pcap
streams = `tshark -r #{in_filename} -T fields -e tcp.stream | sort -n
    | uniq`.split("\n")
streams.shift

p streams.count.to_s + " streams found."

# convert pcaps tp pdml separated by tcp.stream
p "Splitting..."
bar = ProgressBar.create(:total => streams.count)
streams.each do |stream|
  `tshark -r #{in_filename} -T pdml -Y "tcp.stream==#{stream.to_s}"
      >> pdml/#{in_filename}-#{stream.to_s}.pdml`
  bar.increment
end

p "Done."

# create XES file
```

```ruby
open("pcml/file_filename.xes", 'w') do |file|

  # write XES header
  file << "<?xml version=\"1.0\" encoding=\"UTF-8\"?>\n"
  file << "<log xes.version=\"1.0\" xmlns=\"http://www.xes-standard.org\" xes.creator=\"Matthias Leeb\">\n"

  file << "  <extension name=\"Concept\" prefix=\"concept\" uri=\"http://www.xes-standard.org/concept.xesext\"/>\n"
  file << "  <extension name=\"Lifecycle\" prefix=\"lifecycle\" uri=\"http://www.xes-standard.org/lifecycle.xesext\"/>\n"
  file << "  <extension name=\"Time\" prefix=\"time\" uri=\"http://www.xes-standard.org/time.xesext\"/>\n"
  file << "  <extension name=\"Organizational\" prefix=\"org\" uri=\"http://www.xes-standard.org/org.xesext\"/>\n"

  file << "  <global scope=\"trace\">\n"
  file << "    <string key=\"concept:name\" value=\"name\"/>\n"
  file << "  </global>\n"

  file << "  <global scope=\"event\">\n"
  file << "    <string key=\"concept:name\" value=\"name\"/>\n"
  file << "    <string key=\"lifecycle:transition\" value=\"transition\"/>\n"
  file << "    <string key=\"org:resource\" value=\"resource\"/>\n"
  file << "    <date key=\"time:timestamp\" value=\"2011-04-13T14:02:31.199+02:00\"/>\n"
  file << "    <string key=\"activity\" value=\"string\"/>\n"
  file << "    <string key=\"Resource\" value=\"string\"/>\n"
  file << "    <string key=\"concept:name\" value=\"string\"/>\n"
  file << "    <string key=\"org:resource\" value=\"string\"/>\n"
  file << "  </global>\n"
```

```ruby
file << "..<classifier_name=\"Activity\"_key=\"concept:name\"/>_\n"
file << "..<classifier_name=\"Resource\"_keys=\"org:resource\"/>_\n"
file << "..<string_key=\"lifecycle:model\"_value=\"standard\"/>_\n"
file << "..<string_key=\"creator\"_value=\"Matthias_Leeb\"/>_\n"


number = 0
p "Start_writing_XES_..."
bar = ProgressBar.create(:total => streams.count)

# iterate streams
streams.each do |trace|
  number += 1
  doc = Nokogiri::XML(File.open("pcap/#{in_filename}-#{trace_ip_at.
    .xml"))

  if doc.to_s.include? "Hypertext_Transfer_Protocol"

    # begin trace
    file << "..<trace>\n"
    file << "...<string_key=\"concept:name\"_value=\"Stream_" +
      trace.to_s + "\"/>_\n"

    # write events
    packets = doc.xpath('//pdml//packet')
    packets.each do |packet|

      # check if packet is part of HTTP communication
      if packet.to_s.include? "Hypertext_Transfer_Protocol"

        # extract relevant data

        # extract relevant data via xpath
```

```ruby
# whos the actor/resource fo the current activity
actor = packet.xpath('proto[@name="ip"]/field[@name="ip.sr
  "]/@show').to_s + ":" + packet.xpath('proto[@name="tcp
  "]/field[@name="tcp.srcport"]/@show').to_s
# packet/activity arrival time
epoch = packet.xpath('proto[@name="frame"]/field[@name="
  frame.time_epoch"]/@show').to_s
# extract activity
activity = packet.xpath('proto[@name="http"]/field[1]/@show
  ').to_s.chomp("\r\n").upcase

# bring epoch time to format for XES
timestamp = DateTime.strptime(epoch.to_s, '%s').strftime('%
  Y-%m-%dT%H:%M:%S.%3N:z').gsub('000', ('%.3f' % epoch).
  to_s.split('.').last).to_s

# write event
file << "<event>\n"
file << "<string key=\"lifecycle:transition\" value
  =\"complete\"/>\n"

# if activity is GET or POST cut off information
if (activity.include?("GET") || activity.include?("POST"))
  file << "<string key=\"concept:name\" value=\"" +
    activity.split(' ').first + "\"/>\n"
  file << "<string key=\"Activity\" value=\"" +
    activity.split(' ').first + "\"/>\n"
else
  file << "<string key=\"concept:name\" value=\"" +
    activity + "\"/>\n"
  file << "<string key=\"Activity\" value=\"" +
    activity + "\"/>\n"
```

```
     end
     file << "         <string_key=\"org:resource\"_value=\"" +
        actor + "\">\n"
     file << "         <date_key=\"time:timestamp\"_value=\"" +
        timestamp + "\"/>\n"
     file << "         <string_key=\"Resource\"_value=\"" + actor +
           "\"/>\n"

     file << "        </event>\n"

     end

   end
   # close trace
   file << "    </trace>\n"
   bar.increment
   end

  end

  # write XES footer
  file << "</log>"
end

# Delete unnecessary pdml files
p "Cleaning_up..."
`rm pdml/*.pdml`
p "DONE."
```

Listing C.2: http_pcap2xes.rb

## C.3. Script tcp_splitPcaps2xes.rb

```
#!/usr/bin/env ruby

require 'rubygems'
```

```ruby
require '...............'
require '......'
require '......'
require '......'
require '......................'

# check number of arguments
if 1 < ARGV.size
  STDERR << "....................................."
  exit(2)
end


capture_files = `find #{ARGV[0]} -name "*.pcap"`.split("\n")


number_of_arguments = capture_files.size
p "........" + number_of_arguments.to_s + "..............................."

# create XES file
p "O........................"
open(".............", '..') do |file|

  # write XES header
  file << "<?xml version=\"1.0\" encoding=\"UTF-8\"?>\n"
  file << "<log xes.version=\"1.0\" xmlns=\"http://www.xes-standard.
    org\" xes.creator=\"Matthias Leeb\">\n"

  file << "  <extension name=\"Concept\" prefix=\"concept\" uri=\"
    http://www.xes-standard.org/concept.xesext\">\n"
  file << "  <extension name=\"Lifecycle\" prefix=\"lifecycle\" uri
    =\"http://www.xes-standard.org/lifecycle.xesext\"/>\n"
  file << "  <extension name=\"Time\" prefix=\"time\" uri=\"http://
    www.xes-standard.org/time.xesext\"/>\n"
```

```
file << "__<extension_name=\"Organisational\"_prefix=\"org\"_uri=\"
         http://www.xes-standard.org/org.xesext\"/>\n"


file << "__<global_scope=\"trace\">\n"
file << "___<string_key=\"concept:name\"_value=\"name\"/>\n"
file << "__</global>\n"


file << "__<global_scope=\"event\">\n"
file << "___<string_key=\"concept:name\"_value=\"name\"/>\n"
file << "___<string_key=\"lifecycle:transition\"_value=\"
         transition\"/>\n"
file << "___<string_key=\"org:resource\"_value=\"resource\"/>\n"
file << "___<date_key=\"time:timestamp\"_value=\"2011-04-11T14
         :02:31.199+02:00\"/>\n"
file << "___<string_key=\"Activity\"_value=\"string\"/>\n"
file << "___<string_key=\"Resource\"_value=\"string\"/>\n"
file << "___<string_key=\"concept:name\"_value=\"string\"/>\n"
file << "___<string_key=\"org:resource\"_value=\"string\"/>\n"
file << "__</global>\n"


file << "__<classifier_name=\"Activity\"_keys=\"concept:name\"/>\n"
file << "__<classifier_name=\"Resource\"_keys=\"org:resource\"/>\n"
file << "__<string_key=\"lifecycle:model\"_value=\"standard\"/>\n"
file << "__<string_key=\"creator\"_value=\"Matthias_Leeb\"/>\n"


# convert pcaps tp pdml separated by tcp.stream
p "Processing_captures_and_writing_XES..."
bar = ProgressBar.create(:total => number_of_arguments)
number = 1
capture_files.each do |pcaps|
  # 'tshark -r #{pcaps} -T pdml >> tmp.pdml'
  temp_pdml = 'tshark -r #{pcaps} -T pdml'
```

```ruby
# write events
# doc = Nokogiri::XML(File.open("tmp.pdml"))
doc = Nokogiri::XML(temp_pdml)


# check if pdml includes a complete TCP stream
if ((doc.to_s.include?("             ")) && (doc.to_s.include?("
      ")) || (doc.to_s.include?("            ")))
  # begin trace
  file << "            "
  file << "                                                         " +
    sprintf("      ",number) + "        "


  packets = doc.xpath('                ')
  packet_number = 0
  initiator = ""


  packets.each do |packet|
    # Check if packet is part of a TCP connection
    if packet.to_s.include?                                       
      # count packets in stream
      packet_number = packet_number + 1


      # extract relevant data via xpath
      # whos the actor/resource fo the current activity
      actor = packet.xpath(                                      
        "       ").to_s + ": " + packet.xpath(                   
        "                          ").to_s
      # packet/activity arrival time
      epoch = packet.xpath(                                      
             "                           ").to_s
      # extract activity
```

```
h_activity = packet.xpath(                                    ).to_s


# remove unnecessary characters from TCP flag
activity = h_activity.slice(h_activity.index(   )+1 ..
   h_activity.index(   )-1)
# bring epoch time to format for XES
timestamp = DateTime.strptime(epoch.to_s,      ).strftime(
                         ).gsub(      , (       % epoch).
   to_s.split(   ).last).to_s


# Who initiated the connection? -> Sender of first packet
   in stream
if packet_number < 2
   initiator = packet.xpath(
                    ).to_s +      + packet.xpath(
                         ).to_s
end


# write event
file << "            event   \n"
file << "            string key                              value
                   complete    \n"


# distinguish between activities of the two actors by
   leading X
if actor.eql?(initiator)
   file << "            string key  "concept:name" value " " +
      activity + " \  \n"
   file << "            string key  "Activity" value " " +
      activity + " \  \n"
else
```

```ruby
      file << "          <string_key=\"concept:name\"_value=\"x" +
        activity + " \"/>\n"
      file << "          <string_key=\"Activity\"_value=\"x" +
        activity + "\" >\n"
    end


    file << "          <string_key=\"org:resource\"_value=\"\"" +
      actor + "\"/>\n"
    file << "          <date_key=\"time:timestamp\"_value=\"\"" +
      timestamp + "\"/>\n"
    file << "          <string_key=\"Resource\"_value=\"" + actor +
      "\" >\n"

    file << "          </event>\n"
    # event closed
  end


  end


  # close trace
  file << "      </trace>\n"
end


#delete temporary pdml file
# `rm tmp.pdml`
number = number + 1
bar.increment
end


# write XES footer
file << "</log>"
number = number - 1
p "Included_" + number.to_s + "_TCP_streams_to_results.xes_!"
```

```
end
```

Listing C.3: tcp_splitPcaps2xes.rb

# D. Glossary

aig    average information gain. 60, 61, 66

BI    Business Intelligence. 1
BPM    Business Process Management. 1, 6, 7, 67
BPMN    Business Process Model and Notation. 24

DWS    Disjunctive Workflow Schema. 29

ERP    Enterprise Resource Planning. 1, 2
ETL    Extract, Transform, Load. 4, 5, 33, 38, 42, 45, 53, 55, 66, 68, 69

FSM    Finite State Machine. 28, 29

GB    Gigabyte. 34, 59, 68
GUI    Graphical User Interface. 62

HTTP    Hypertext Transfer Protocol. 4, 5, 17, 39, 55–57, 66, 68, 97

IPS    Intrusion Prevention System. 17
Iv    Information value. 60, 61, 66

MB    Megabyte. 57

PAIS    Process-Aware Information System. 7, 19

PCAP    Packet CAPture. 35, 36, 42, 59, 68, 69

PDML    Packet Details Markup Language. 35, 36, 38, 39, 42, 46, 56, 68, 69, 96

PNML    Petri Net Markup Language. 9, 31

SOX    Sarbanes-Oxley Act. 2

SSD    Solid-State-Drive. 59, 68

TCP    Transmission Control Protocol. 4, 5, 17, 25, 33, 35, 36, 38, 39, 42–47, 49–56, 59, 60, 68, 69, 97

UDP    User Datagram Protocol. 56, 59

WFM    WorkFlow Management. 2, 6

WF-net    WorkFlow net. 26

WoPeD    Workflow Petri Net Designer. 9, 76

XES    eXtensible Event Stream. 4, 22, 24, 39, 42, 44, 45, 52, 68, 96, 97

XML    eXtensible Markup Language. 24, 38, 52, 68

XPath    XML Path Language. 38

YAWL    Yet Another Workflow Language. 9, 24

# List of Listings

# List of Figures

# List of Tables

# Bibliography

[1] W. M. P. van der Aalst, D. Hauschildt, and H. M. W. Verbeek. "A Petri-net-based Tool to Analyze Workflows." In: *Proceedings of Petri Nets in System Engineering (PNSE'97).* FBI-HH-B-205/97. University of Hamburg, 1997, pp. 78–90. http://www.informatik.uni-hamburg.de /TGI/aktuelles/pnse97/papers/aalst.ps.gz.

[2] Wil MP van der Aalst, Mariska Netjes, and Hajo A Reijers. "Supporting the full BPM life-cycle using process mining and intelligent redesign." In: *Contemporary Issues in Database Design and Information Systems Devevelopment* (2007), pp. 100–132.

[3] NETRESEC AB. http://www.netresec.com/?page=SplitCap (last access: 06/23/2015).

[4] NETRESEC AB. http://sourceforge.net/projects/splitcap/files/lates t (last access: 06/23/2015).

[5] About.com. http://linux.about.com/cs/linux101/g/process1parproc.htm (last access: 05/23/2015).

[6] Student Victor Anthony Arrascue Ayala. "Distribution list." In: (2012).

[7] Eric Badouel and Philippe Darondeau. "Theory of regions." In: *Lectures on Petri Nets I: Basic Models.* Springer, 1998, pp. 529–586.

[8] Ruby community. (2015, 1). https://www.ruby-lang.org/en/ (last access: 04/21/2015).

[9] Weidong Cui, Jayanthkumar Kannan, and Helen J Wang. "Discoverer: Automatic Protocol Reverse Engineering from Network Traces." In: *USENIX Security.* 2007, pp. 199–212.

[10] Thomas H Davenport. *Process innovation: reengineering work through information technology.* Harvard Business Press, 2013.

[11] N. Davids. http://noahdavids.org/self_published/split_pcap.html (last access: 05/30/2015).

[12] UNB's Communications & Marketing department. http://www.unb.ca/ (last access: 06/02/2015).

[13] UNB's Communications & Marketing department. `http://ge128m21.cs.unb.ca/data sets/iscx2012/` (last access: 06/02/2015).

[14] Boudewijn F van Dongen, AK Alves De Medeiros, and Lijie Wen. "Process mining: Overview and outlook of petri net discovery algorithms." In: *Transactions on Petri Nets and Other Models of Concurrency II*. Springer, 2009, pp. 225–242.

[15] Boudewijn F van Dongen and Wil MP Van der Aalst. "Multi-phase process mining: Aggregating instance graphs into EPCs and Petri nets." In: *PNCWB 2005 workshop*. Citeseer. 2005, pp. 35–58.

[16] Boudewijn F van Dongen et al. *An iterative algorithm for applying the theory of regions in process mining*. Beta, Research School for Operations Management and Logistics, 2007.

[17] Marlon Dumas, Wil Van der Aalst, and Arthur ter Hofstede. *Process-Aware Information Systems*.

[18] Process Mining Group TU Eindhoven. `http://www.processmining.org/online/fr equencyabstractionminer` (last access: 05/03/2015).

[19] Process Mining Group TU Eindhoven. `http://www.processmining.org/online/fu zzyminer` (last access: 05/03/2015).

[20] Process Mining Group TU Eindhoven. `http://www.processmining.org/online/co ntrolflowdiscovery` (last access: 05/03/2015).

[21] Process Mining Group TU Eindhoven. `http://www.promtools.org/doku.php` (last access: 05/30/2015).

[22] Process Mining Group TU Eindhoven. `https://svn.win.tue.nl/trac/prom/brows er/Documentation` (last access: 05/30/2015).

[23] Process Mining Group TU Eindhoven. `http://www.promtools.org/doku.php?id=p rom641` (last access: 05/30/2015).

[24] Process Mining Group TU Eindhoven. (2015, 1). `http://www.processmining.org/re search/start` (last access: 01/15/2015).

[25] Process Mining Group TU Eindhoven. (2015, 1). `http://www.promtools.org/doku.p hp` (last access: 01/15/2015).

[26] R Fielding et al. "RFC 2616." In: *Hypertext Transfer Protocol–HTTP/1.1* 2.1 (1999), pp. 2–2.

[27] The Apache Software Foundation. `http://httpd.apache.org` (last access: 05/23/2015).

[28] The R Foundation. `http://www.r-project.org/` (last access: 07/01/2015).

[29]  The R Foundation. `http://cran.r-project.org/manuals.html` (last access: 07/01/2015).

[30]  The R Foundation. `http://cran.at.r-project.org/` (last access: 07/01/2015).

[31]  The YAWL Foundation. `http://yawlfoundation.org/` (last access: 06/08/2015).

[32]  Wireshark Foundation. `https://www.wireshark.org/docs/man-pages/tshark.html` (last access: 04/24/2015).

[33]  Wireshark Foundation. `https://www.wireshark.org` (last access: 04/24/2015).

[34]  Wireshark Foundation. `https://www.wireshark.org/download.html` (last access: 04/24/2015).

[35]  Wireshark Foundation. `https://www.wireshark.org/docs/wsug%5C_html%5C_chunked/index.html` (last access: 04/24/2015).

[36]  Thomas Freytag. `http://www.woped.org` (last access: 04/24/2015).

[37]  Thomas Freytag. `http://woped.dhbw-karlsruhe.de/woped/?page_id=22` (last access: 04/24/2015).

[38]  Walid Gaaloul et al. "Mining workflow patterns through event-data analysis." In: *Applications and the Internet Workshops, 2005. Saint Workshops 2005. The 2005 Symposium on*. IEEE. 2005, pp. 226–229.

[39]  Gianluigi Greco et al. "Mining expressive process models by clustering workflow traces." In: *Advances in Knowledge Discovery and Data Mining*. Springer, 2004, pp. 52–62.

[40]  Process Mining Group. `http://www.rapidprom.org` (last access: 05/18/2015).

[41]  Christian W Günther and Wil MP Van Der Aalst. "Fuzzy mining–adaptive process simplification based on multi-perspective metrics." In: *Business Process Management*. Springer, 2007, pp. 328–343.

[42]  Christian W. Günther and Eric Verbeek. *XES*. 2014-03. `http://www.xes-standard.org/_media/xes/xesstandarddefinition-2.0.pdf` (visited on 01/23/2015).

[43]  Craig Hunt. *TCP/IP network administration*. Vol. 2. " O'Reilly Media, Inc.", 2002.

[44]  Apple Inc. `https://www.apple.com/osx/` (last access: 04/24/2015).

[45]  RapidMiner Inc. `https://rapidminer.com/rapidminer-5-0/` (last access: 05/18/2015).

[46] WebFinance Inc. `http://www.businessdictionary.com/definition/busines s-process.html` (last access: 05/18/2015).

[47] JetBRAINS. `https://www.jetbrains.com/ruby/` (last access: 04/24/2015).

[48] JetBRAINS. `https://www.jetbrains.com/` (last access: 04/24/2015).

[49] Henry J Johansson et al. *Business process reengineering: Breakpoint strategies for market dominance*. Wiley Chichester, 1993.

[50] Fluxicon Process Laboratories. `http://fluxicon.com/disco/` (last access: 05/18/2015).

[51] Fluxicon Process Laboratories. `http://fluxicon.com/camp/2012/` (last access: 05/23/2015).

[52] Fluxicon Process Laboratories. `http://fluxicon.com/camp/2013/` (last access: 05/23/2015).

[53] Fluxicon Process Laboratories. `http://fluxicon.com/camp/2014/` (last access: 05/23/2015).

[54] Fluxicon Process Laboratories. `http://fluxicon.com/camp/2015/` (last access: 06/20/2015).

[55] Fluxicon Process Laboratories. `http://fluxicon.com/disco/` (last access: 05/19/2015).

[56] Zhiqiang Lin et al. "Automatic Protocol Format Reverse Engineering through Context-Aware Monitored Execution." In: *NDSS*. Vol. 8. 2008, pp. 1–15.

[57] Ana Karla A de Medeiros, Wil MP van der Aalst, and AJMM Weijters. "Workflow mining: Current status and future directions." In: *On the move to meaningful internet systems 2003: Coopis, doa, and odbase*. Springer, 2003, pp. 389–406.

[58] Ana Karla A de Medeiros, Anton JMM Weijters, and Wil MP van der Aalst. "Genetic process mining: an experimental evaluation." In: *Data Mining and Knowledge Discovery* 14.2 (2007), pp. 245–304.

[59] Ana Karla Alves de Medeiros. "Genetic process mining." PhD thesis. Technische Universiteit Eindhoven, 2006. `http://alexandria.tue.nl/extra2/200611953.pdf`.

[60] perl.org. `https://www.perl.org` (last access: 05/28/2015).

[61] perl.org. `https://www.perl.org/docs.html` (last access: 05/28/2015).

[62] perl.org. `https://www.perl.org/get.html` (last access: 05/28/2015).

[63] Jon Postel. *TCP: Transmission Control Protocol.* Tech. rep. RFC 0793, IETF Network Working Group, 1981. Available: http://www. ietf. org/rfc/rfc0793. txt, 1981.

[64] Inc. Headquarters RapidMiner. `http://sourceforge.net/projects/rapidminer/` (last access: 07/04/2015).

[65] Inc. Headquarters RapidMiner. `http://docs.rapidminer.com/studio/getting-s tarted/` (last access: 07/04/2015).

[66] A. Rozinat. `http://fluxicon.com/disco/files/Disco-Tour.pdf` (last access: 05/19/2015).

[67] A. Rozinat. `http://fluxicon.com/disco/files/Disco-User-Guide.pdf` (last access: 05/19/2015).

[68] A. Rozinat. `http://fluxicon.com/academic/material/files/Installation .pdf` (last access: 05/19/2015).

[69] Anne Rozinat et al. "The need for a process mining evaluation framework in research and practice." In: *Business Process Management Workshops.* Springer. 2008, pp. 84–89.

[70] Anne Rozinat et al. *Towards an evaluation framework for process mining algorithms.* Beta, Research School for Operations Management and Logistics, 2007.

[71] RStudio. `http://www.rstudio.com/` (last access: 07/01/2015).

[72] RStudio. `https://support.rstudio.com/hc/en-us` (last access: 07/01/2015).

[73] RStudio. `http://www.rstudio.com/products/rstudio/download/` (last access: 07/01/2015).

[74] A.S. Tanenbaum. *Computer Networks.* Computer Networks S. 3. Prentice Hall PTR, 2003. ISBN: 9780130661029. `http://books.google.de/books?id=Pd-z64SJRBAC.`

[75] RapidMiner - Prom 6 Extension Team. `http://www.win.tue.nl/r%CC%83mans/Rapi dMiner/doku.php?id=wiki:documentation` (last access: 07/04/2015).

[76] RapidMiner - Prom 6 Extension Team. `http://www.win.tue.nl/r%CC%83mans/Rapi dMiner/lib/exe/fetch.php?media=wiki:tutorial%5C_rm5%5C_prom6exte nsion.pdf` (last access: 07/04/2015).

[77] unknown. `http://gd.tuwien.ac.at/.vhost/analyzer.polito.it/30alpha /docs/dissectors/PDMLSpec.htm` (last access: 06/20/2015).

[78] Wil Van Der Aalst. *Process mining: discovery, conformance and enhancement of business processes.* Springer Science & Business Media, 2011.

[79] Wil Van Der Aalst et al. "Process mining manifesto." In: *Business process management workshops.* Springer. 2012, pp. 169–194.

[80] Eric Verbeek. http://www.win.tue.nl/~hverbeek/doku.php?id=projects:p rom:plug-ins:conversion:petrify (last access: 07/13/2015).

[81] Jianmin Wang et al. "An empirical evaluation of process mining algorithms based on structural and behavioral similarities." In: *Proceedings of the 27th Annual ACM Symposium on Applied Computing.* ACM. 2012, pp. 211–213.

[82] Philip Weber et al. "A framework for comparing process mining algorithms." In: *GCC Conference and Exhibition (GCC), 2011 IEEE.* IEEE. 2011, pp. 625–628.

[83] AJMM Weijters, Wil MP van Der Aalst, and AK Alves De Medeiros. "Process mining with the heuristics miner-algorithm." In: *Technische Universiteit Eindhoven, Tech. Rep. WP* 166 (2006), pp. 1–34.

[84] AJMM Weijters, Wil MP van Der Aalst, and AK Alves De Medeiros. "Process mining with the heuristics miner-algorithm." In: *Technische Universiteit Eindhoven, Tech. Rep. WP* 166 (2006), pp. 1–34.

[85] Lijie Wen et al. "A novel approach for process mining based on event types." In: *Journal of Intelligent Information Systems* 32.2 (2009), pp. 163–190.

[86] Lijie Wen et al. "Mining process models with non-free-choice constructs." In: *Data Mining and Knowledge Discovery* 15.2 (2007), pp. 145–180.

[87] Agnes Werner-Stark, Miklós Gerzson, and Katalin M Hangos. "Discrete event model structure identification using process mining." In: *Proceedings of the IASTED International Conference Modelling, Identification, and Control (MIC 2011), Innsbruck, Austria.* 2011, pp. 228–233.

[88] Theun van der Wiel and Boudewijn van Dongen. *ILP-Miner.* 2010-06. (Visited on 05/03/2015).